Pray *Without* CEASING

IVERINE JAMES

ISBN 979-8-89130-597-7 (paperback)
ISBN 979-8-89130-598-4 (digital)

Christian Faith Publishing
832 Park Avenue
Meadville, PA 16335
www.christianfaithpublishing.com

Unless otherwise stated, scriptures are taken from the New King James Version (NKJV).

Printed in the United States of America

Lord, I worship you and glorify your Holy name. Lord, I come to you with everything in the open. Lord, I lay everything down ready to be blessed and filled with your presence as I relax and feel the relief of being totally open to you. Lord, you know everything about me; nothing is hidden.

Lord, lead me to be kind to others with the joy, love, and peace of Jesus in me. Lord, I thank you for your living Word. Lord, I thank you that there is no limit to the depth of intimacy I can experience with you. Thank you, Lord, in Jesus name, Amen.

* * * * *

Lord, I thank you that you are the living God. I thank you that a lasting, abundant life can only be found in you alone. Lord, I pray that I will identify more and more fully with you and that my life will become increasingly more like yours. Lord, I pray that your light will shine through me as I walk in your presence.

Delight yourself also in the Lord,
and he will give you the desires of your
heart. (Psalm 37:4)

Thank you, Lord, in Jesus name, Amen.

* * * * *

Lord, I thank you for your presence. Lord, I pray that you will lead me to expose and expel any rebellious ways.

Holy Spirit, increase my awareness of any resentful feelings.

Lord, lead me in the light of your presence. I pray that you will free me from every sinful way. Lord, I submit to your leading over my life, and I rejoice in your sovereignty.

> The word of God is alive and active.
> Sharper than any double-edged sword,
> it penetrates even to dividing soul and
> spirit, joints and marrow; it judges the
> thoughts and attitudes of the heart.
> (Hebrews 4:12)

* * * * *

Holy Father, I pray this morning that my whole attention will turn to you so that I can feel the light of your presence shining over me. Help me to open my mind and heart to receive your heavenly smile of approval.

Holy Spirit, I pray that you will wash me with the living Word of God so that I can experience the joy of God within me.

Thank you, Lord Jesus, that you are my refuge and strength, in Jesus name, Amen.

* * * * *

Lord, I thank you for leading me to lie down in green pastures of peace and rest in the presence of my shepherd.

Lord, I pray that you will lead me into stillness and allow me to take time to seek your direction for my life. Lord, I thank you that you called me to walk with you down the path of peace. Lord, I put my trust in you, and thank you for showering me with your peace, in Jesus name, Amen.

* * * * *

Lord, I thank you that you are God with me throughout all eternity. Lord, I thank you for your presence, which is a continual source of joy, springing up and flowing out in streams of abundant life.

Thank you that you are Immanuel God with us, and that Jesus, the Lord, saves.

Lord, lead me to come to you with everything in the open. Lord, I thank you for your loving presence that can heal me and train me to trust you more. Thank you, Lord, in Jesus name, Amen.

* * * * *

Lord, I thank you that you are the great I am. Thank you for smoothing my heart and giving me joy. Lord, you are all I need, and I thank you that I am complete in your presence. Lord, I thank you for showing compassion on me and shining your face upon me.

> There is a time for everything and a
> season for every activity under the heav-
> ens. (Ecclesiastes 3:1)

Thank you, Lord, in Jesus name, Amen.

* * * * *

Lord, I thank you for the awareness of your presence that led me the way to go. Lord, I pray that you will lead me to live close to you and stay in communication with you. Lord, I thank you that you are the creator of the universe. Lord, I pray that you will lead me to follow your guiding presence.

> And my God will meet all your
> needs according to the riches of his Glory
> in Christ Jesus. (Philippians 4:19)

Thank you, Lord, in Jesus name, Amen.

* * * * *

> My help comes from the Lord, the
> maker of heaven and earth. (Psalm 121:2)

> The name of the Lord is a fortified
> tower; the righteous run to it and are
> safe. (Proverbs 18:10)

Lord, I thank you that my help comes from you. I pray that you will give me the strength to see that when I am going through any situation, it is an opportunity to grow in grace.

Holy Father, I pray for a heart of forgiveness. I pray that I will keep my focus on you because it is your view of me that counts.

Thank you, Lord, for clothing me in your righteousness and Holiness. Thank you, Lord, that I was bought by the blood of Jesus Christ. Thank you, Lord, for the peace and love that you have poured out into my heart by your Holy Spirit.

Holy Spirit, I pray that you increase my awareness of the peace of God's presence in my life as I whisper, "Your Holy name Jesus, Jesus, Jesus."

Thank you, Lord, in Jesus name, Amen.

* * * * *

Lord, as I sit in your presence, I pray that you will lead me to be still. Lord, I pray that you will quiet my mind from anything around me and keep my focus on you so that I can hear from you.

Thank you, Lord, that as I sit in your presence, you equip me for the days ahead of me.

Lord, I thank you for clothing me in the robe of righteousness. Lord, I want to know you more and love you more. Lord, I pray that you will live through me and transform me into your likeness, in Jesus name, Amen.

* * * * *

Lord, I thank you for being with me. I thank you that you will never leave me or forsake me.

Lord, my desire as your sheep is to hear your voice continually for you are the ever-present shepherd.

Holy Spirit, lead me in quietness to hear the voice of God.

Thank you Lord, that, I can express my concern to you freely. Help me become aware of your loving presence. Thank you, Lord, in Jesus name, Amen.

> Trust in him at all times, you peo-
> ple; pour out your hearts to him, for God
> is our refuge. (Psalm 62:8)

* * * * *

Lord, I pray that you will lead me to listen to you.

Holy Spirit, lead me to respond appropriately to the voice of the Lord.

Holy Spirit, I pray that you will think through me, live through me, and love through me.

Lord, I thank you that my own being is alive within the person of the Holy Spirit.

Holy Spirit, I pray that you will empower my listening and speaking so that streams of living water flow through me to others.

Lord, help me to be a channel of love, joy, and peace. Thank you, Lord, in Jesus name, Amen.

* * * * *

Lord, I thank you for your loving-kindness and tender mercy.

Holy Spirit, I pray that you will lead me. My heart's desire is to be aware of your presence and walk closer to you continually.

Lord, help me to see myself the way you see me. Lord, I rejoice in you as you increasingly light up my life with your presence.

Holy Spirit, help me and lead me to have a mind like Christ.

Therefore, holy brothers and sisters, who share in the heavenly calling, fix your thoughts on Jesus, whom we acknowledge as our apostle and high priest of our confession, Christ Jesus. (Hebrews 3:1)

Thank you, Lord, in Jesus name, Amen.

* * * * *

Lord, I pray that you will lead me to grow strong in the light of your presence. Lord, I thank you for your power that is always available to me.

Holy Spirit, I pray that you will lead me, as the light of your love fills my heart.

The Lord appeared to us in the past, saying, "I have loved you with an everlasting love; I have drawn you with unfailing kindness." (Jeremiah 31:3)

Thank you, Lord, in Jesus name, Amen.

* * * * *

Lord, I thank you that I can come to you, talk to you, and have a relationship with you. I thank you because talking to you blesses and strengthens our relationship. Lord, I pray that you will lead me to have a thankful heart. Lord, I thank you for the gift of the Holy Spirit that led me to repentance.

Thank you that my past, present, and future are under the blood of Jesus. Thank you, Lord, in Jesus name, Amen.

> If our hearts condemn us, we know
> that God is greater than our hearts and
> knows all things. (1 John 3:20)

* * * * *

Lord, I thank you for your presence. Thank you for leading me to walk with you peacefully throughout each day. Lord, I thank you that I was designed for deep dependence on you, my Shepherd, my King. Lord, I thank you that when I don't know what to do, I will wait on you as you open the way before me.

Thank you, Lord, that you know what is best for me. Thank you, Lord, for giving me strength and blessing me with peace. Thank you, Lord, for your grace is sufficient for me.

Thank you, Lord, in Jesus name, Amen.

* * * * *

Lord, I thank you for calling me to live in your presence. Lord, I pray that you will lead me to put all my trust in you and enjoy your presence.

Thank you for being with me and watching over me. Thank you for meeting all my needs according to your glorious riches. Thank you for knowing that nothing in creation will be able to separate me from your love.

> Oh, taste and see that the Lord is
> good; blessed is the one who puts trust in
> him. (Psalm 34:8)

Thank you, Lord, in Jesus name, Amen.

* * * * *

Holy Father, I pray that you will lead me to please you above all else.

Lord, I pray that you will help me to strive to please you at all times and to keep in close communication with you. Lord, I pray that your presence will be my deepest delight. Lord, lead me to always please you. Lord, I pray that I will delight myself in you more and more and seek your presence in all I do and say.

I pray that my life will reflect you at all times. Lord, I thank you for your peace. I receive your peace in Jesus name, Amen.

> In the same way, let your light shine before others, that they may see your good deeds and glorify your Father in heaven. (Matthew 5:16)

* * * * *

Lord, I thank you that you call me to be all yours. Thank you that I belong to the King of Glory. Thank you for filling me with the overflow of love, joy, and peace. Lord, I worship you in the beauty of holiness. Lord, I pray that you will clean out anything that is not of you from within me.

Holy Spirit, I pray that you will take full control of my life.

Lord, I thank you for training me to depend on you alone and find fulfillment in your presence. Thank you, Lord, in Jesus name, Amen.

* * * * *

Lord, I thank you. Lord, I praise you. Lord, I glorify your Holy name. Lord, when I look back and see how you protect me, guide me, provide for me, and strengthen me, Holy Father, I praise you and thank you, Lord, for the blood of Jesus. Thank you for saving me, Lord. I thank you that you remain the same throughout time and eternity.

I bow down to you, Lord, and thank you for your presence.

> Trust in the Lord with all your heart and lean not on your own understanding. In all your ways, acknowledge him, and he shall direct your path. (Proverbs 3:5)

In Jesus name, Amen.

* * * * *

> So we make it our goal to please him, whether we are at home in the body or away from it. (2 Corinthians 5:9)

Lord, lead me to focus my entire being on living in your presence. Lord, I thank you that while I am in your presence, you are molding my mind and cleansing my heart. Lord, I thank you for recreating me into the one you designed me to be. Lord, I pray that you will lead me to bring everything to you and fill my time with prayer and praise. Lord, lead me to seek you in every aspect of my life.

Thank you, Lord. In Jesus name, I pray, Amen.

* * * * *

Lord, I thank you that I can bask in the luxury of being fully understood and unconditionally loved by you.

Holy Spirit, I pray that you will lead me to see myself as the Lord sees me, radiant in the righteousness of God and cleansed by the blood of Jesus.

Lord, I thank you for the gift of the Holy Spirit within me.

Holy Spirit, I need your help as I go through each day. Thank you, Lord, in Jesus name, Amen.

> But I trust in your unfailing love,
> and my heart rejoices in your salvation. I
> will sing the Lord's praise, for he has been
> good to me. (Psalm 13:5–6)

* * * * *

Father God, I thank you that there is now no condemnation for those who are in Christ Jesus, who do not walk according to the flesh but according to the Spirit.

Lord, I thank you that you died to set me free.

Holy Spirit, I pray that you will lead me to live freely in our Lord and Savior, Jesus Christ, and to walk along the path of freedom.

Lord, lead me to fix my mind and heart firmly on you. Lord, lead me to listen to you, the voice of truth, and thank you for the divine transformation that you are doing in me daily. Thank you for leading me into green pastures and guiding me on the paths of righteousness.

Thank you, Lord, in Jesus name, Amen.

* * * * *

Lord, I pray that you will lead me to come to you and rest in your peace. Thank you, Lord, for shining your face upon me. Thank you for your peace that passes all understanding.

Lord, I thank you that I can rest and don't have to try to figure things out all by myself. Thank you for the Holy Spirit that led me into righteousness.

Lord, I come to you and relax in your presence, the one who knows everything. Thank you, Lord, that I was designed to live in close communication with you.

Holy Spirit, I pray that you will give me words of grace as I live in the light of your presence. In Jesus name, Amen.

* * * * *

Lord, I pray that you will lead me to always be thankful. Lord, I thank you for blessing me with spiritual gifts that flow from you. Lord, I thank you that my thankfulness enables me to communicate intimately with you. Lord, I pray that you will lead me to rejoice in you, my Savior and King.

Thank you, Lord, that you are my refuge and strength.

> He brought me out into a spacious place; He rescued me because He delighted in me. (2 Samuel 22:20)

In Jesus name, Amen.

* * * * *

Lord, I pray that you will lead me to sit quietly in your presence as you fill my heart and mind with thankfulness.

Holy Spirit, I pray that you will lead my mind to focus on the cross, where the blood of Jesus was poured out for me.

Thank you, Lord, that nothing will be able to separate me from your love. Lord, I pray that I will always have a heart of gratitude. Lord, I thank you for going before me and planting treasures to brighten my day. Lord, I thank you for your peace. I rejoice in your Holy name, Amen. Hallelujah.

In Jesus name, Amen.

* * * * *

Father God, I thank you for instructing me to give thanks for everything.

Lord, lead me to give thanks regardless of my feelings. Lord, I thank you for giving me peace and joy. Lord, I thank you that my thankfulness opens my heart to your presence and my mind to think the way you think. Lord, thank you for the light of your presence. In Jesus name, Amen.

* * * * *

This is the day which the Lord hath
made; we will rejoice and be glad in it.
(Psalm 118:24)

Lord, I pray for a heart that is always thankful and rejoices. Lord, I thank you that in every situation I can rejoice because the light of your presence is shining on me.

I will offer to thee the sacrifice of
thanksgiving and will call upon the name
of the Lord. (Psalm 116:17)

> Thou art my God, and I will praise
> thee; thou art my God, I will exalt thee.
> (Psalm 118:28)

Thank you, Lord, in Jesus name, Amen.

*   *   *   *   *

Father God, I pray that I will always be thankful. Thank you, Lord, for blessing me. Thank you for saving me and enabling me to see more and more of your glorious riches.

Lord, I praise you. Hallelujah, Hallelujah.

Lord, lead me to focus on you and what you are doing in my life. Open my spiritual eyes to see you. Lord, open the understanding of my heart. Lord, I thank you that I was created to worship you and glorify your holy name.

> And I will pray to the Father, and he
> shall give you another Comforter, that he
> may abide with you forever Amen. (John
> 14:16)

Thank you, Lord, in Jesus name, Amen.

*   *   *   *   *

Father, as I rest in the deep assurance of your unfailing love, I pray that my body, mind, and spirit relax in your presence.

Lord, I release into your hands every situation. Lord, lead me to focus my full attention on you. Lord, I rejoice in you. Lord, I thank you for being my provider, my restorer,

my healer, and my all in all. Lord, I come to you with a sacrifice of gratitude.

> Every good and perfect gift is from
> above, coming down from the father of
> the heavenly light, who does not change
> like shifting shadows. (James 1:17)

In Jesus name, Amen.

* * * * *

Lord, I come to you, thanking you for saving me. Thank you for your abundant blessing on me. Lord, I pray that you will lead me into a deep and intimate relationship with you. Lord, I want to know you more. I want to know your heart. Lord, I pray that my relationship with you will be my primary concern. Lord, lead me to bring everything to you. Lord, I pray that you will show me what is truly import-ant and lead me to seek what you seek. Lord, lead me to love as you do.

Thank you, Lord, that your image and spirit in me are powerful and making me fit for greatness.

Lord, I look to you for strength and guidance. Lord, I pray that I will desire what you desire. Thank you, Lord, King of Glory, in Jesus name, Amen.

* * * * *

Lord, I thank you for loving me with an everlasting love that flows out from the depths of eternity. Lord, I thank you that you knew me before I was born.

Father God, I pray that you will lead me to be still in your presence.

Lord, I pray that you will speak to me and that my heart and mind will be open to hearing you.

> The Lord is my rock, my fortress,
> and my deliverer; my God is my rock in
> whom I take refuge. He is my shield and
> the horn of my salvation, my stronghold.
> (Psalm 18:2)

Thank you, Lord, in Jesus name, Amen.

* * * * *

Lord, I thank you that you are the prince of peace. Lord, I thank you for being my constant companion and that your steadfast peace is always with me.

Holy Father, I pray that I will keep my focus on you that I can experience both your presence and your peace.

Lord, as I walk along the path of peace, I will enjoy the journey in your presence.

Thank you, Lord, for being my Creator, my King, my Savior, and my Shepherd.

Lord, I give you glory in Jesus name, Amen.

> And my God shall supply all your
> needs according to his riches in glory by
> Christ Jesus Amen. (Philippians 4:19)

* * * * *

Lord, I thank you for designing me to need you at all times. Thank you, Lord, for our daily bread and for fulfilling our deep yearning for you. Lord, as I spend time in your presence, my deepest longing is fulfilled. Lord, I rejoice in you, and I thank you for sustaining me. Lord, I praise your Holy name. Thank you, Lord, in Jesus name, Amen.

> I have set the Lord continually
> before me because he is at my right hand.
> I will not be moved. (Psalm 16:8)

Father God, I thank you that you are working on my behalf. Lord, I bring you all my concerns, including my dreams. Lord, lead me to talk to you about everything. I pray that the light of your presence shines upon me. Thank you, Lord, that the creator of the universe wants to have a relationship with me.

> Commit your way to the Lord; trust
> also in him; and he will do it. (Psalm 37:5)

Thank you, Lord, in Jesus name, Amen.

* * * * *

Lord, I thank you for taking care of me and for loving me. Lord, I thank you for the warm security of being in your loving presence. Thank you, Lord, that every detail of my life is under your control and everything fits into a pattern for good for those who love you and are called according to your purpose.

Lord, I thank you that you are close to me and that you constantly work on my behalf. Lord, I pray that I will walk by faith and not by sight, trusting in your majestic presence. Thank you, Lord, in Jesus name, Amen.

* * * * *

Lord, I pray that you will lead me to be holy as you set me apart for your sacred use. Lord, lead me into a quiet moment in your presence. Lord, as I focus my heart and mind on you, I thank you that I have been transformed and I am being recreated into the one I was designed to be as I soak in the light of your presence.

Lord, I thank you for your nearness that strengthens my faith and fills me with peace as I open myself up to receive the many blessings that you have prepared for me as I become a clean temple of the Holy Spirit, in Jesus name, Amen.

* * * * *

Lord, I thank you that I am your child and I rest in you. Lord, I pray that you will lead me to forget about the world and focus on you Immanuel God with us.

I pray that your living presence will envelope me with peace. Thank you, Lord, that you are the same yesterday, today, and forever.

Lord, I pray that I will begin each day alone with you and experience the reality of your presence. Lord, I thank you that as I spend time with you, the way before me, will open up step-by-step.

Lord, my total dependence is on you. Thank you, Lord, in Jesus name, Amen.

* * * * *

Lord, I thank you that you are my savior and that heaven has become my ultimate destination. Thank you, Lord, that the hope of heaven keeps me spiritually alive.

Lord, I thank you that your desire for me is that I may overflow with the hope of the power of the Holy Spirit.

Lord, as I confidently relax in your presence, I find refreshment in the refuge of your everlasting arms. Thank you, Lord, in Jesus name, Amen.

* * * * *

Lord, I thank you for speaking in the depths of my being to be still so that I can hear your voice. Lord, thank you that you speak in a language of love. Thank you, Lord, for your loving words that fill me with life, peace, joy, and hope.

Lord, I pray that you will lead me to live close to you. Thank you, Lord, that you are my first love and my highest priority.

Lord, I seek your presence above all else as I experience peace and joy in full measure. Thank you, Lord, that your glory brightens the world around me, in Jesus name, Amen.

* * * * *

Lord, I come to you with emptiness, knowing that I am complete in you. Lord, as I rest quietly in you, I thank you that your light grows brighter and brighter within me.

Lord, I pray that you will lead me to depend on you in a childlike trust, knowing that you will never leave me or forsake me. Thank you, Lord, that you are from whom all blessings flow. Thank you, Lord, in Jesus name, Amen.

> The thief comes only to steal, kill, and
> destroy; I have come that they may have
> life and have it to the full. (John 10:10)

* * * * *

Lord, I pray that my life will become a praise song to you by proclaiming your glorious presence in the world.

Lord, I thank you for the faith, hope, and love that work together to shield me as I journey through this world.

Thank you for the faith, hope, and love that also keep me close to you.

> But since we belong to the day, let
> us be self-controlled, putting on faith and
> love as a breastplate and the hope of sal-
> vation as a helmet. (1 Thessalonians 5:8)

In Jesus name, Amen.

* * * * *

Lord, I thank you that you have plans for my life. Lord, I thank you for your power and glory and your strength to sustain me. Lord, I thank you that living by faith rather than sight enables me to see your glory. Lord, help me to think my thoughts through and see things from your perspective as I wait in your presence.

> O Lord, you have searched me,
> Lord, and you know me. You know when
> I sit and when I rise; you perceive my
> thoughts from afar. (Psalm 139:1–2)

Thank you, Lord, in Jesus name, Amen.

* * * * *

Thank you, Father God, that you are the King of kings and Lord of lords. Thank you that you are the light, the good shepherd, the vine, my companion, and my friend, the one who will never let go of my hand.

Lord, I worship you in your holy majesty. Lord, I pray that you will lead me to come close to you and rest in your presence. Lord, I thank you for saving me from all sins. Lord, I thank you for living within me.

I rejoice in you and know that your light will shine through me, in Jesus name, Amen.

* * * * *

Lord, I thank you that you are the great I am. Lord, I thank you that you talk to me in the depths of my heart, where you take up residence. Thank you, Lord, that you are Christ in me, the hope of glory.

Thank you, my Lord and Savior, for being alive in me. Lord, I thank you for your glorious gift of salvation. I pray that your peace rules in my heart and mind. Thank you, Lord, in Jesus name, Amen.

> Let us fix our eyes on Jesus, the author and perfector of faith. (Hebrews 12:2)

In Jesus's name, Amen.

* * * * *

Lord, as I wait in your presence, I thank you that the light of your glory shines upon me. Lord, I thank you that your presence transforms every fiber of my being and renews my heart.

Father God, I thank you for sending your only son to save me from sin.

Thank you, Lord, that you became poor so that I might become rich. Hallelujah to your Holy name. Thank you, Lord, in Jesus name, Amen.

> May your unfailing love be my
> comfort, according to your promise to
> your servant. (Psalm 119:76)

* * * * *

Lord, I thank you for your unconditional love. Thank you, Lord, that absolutely nothing in heaven or on earth can cause you to stop loving me.

Thank you, Lord, that your love for me is perfect. Lord, I thank you for your loving presence.

Holy Spirit, I pray that you will empower me to live in the fullness of your presence.

> Therefore, there is now no condem-
> nation for those who are in Christ Jesus,
> who does not walk according to the flesh
> but according to the spirit. (Romans 8:1)

In Jesus name, Amen.

* * * * *

Lord, I pray that you will lead me to be still in your presence so that I will be strengthened. Lord, lead me to walk close to you, depending on your strength and trusting you in every situation. Lord, I pray that you will lead me to walk in the light with you and reflect you in the world. Lord, I pray that you will lead me to tell others about my Lord and Savior, King of Glory, and that they come to know you, in Jesus name, Amen.

* * * * *

Lord, I thank you that you are my refuge, strength, and ever-present help in trouble. Lord, I thank you that I do not need to be afraid of anything because you are always with me, holding my hand and guiding me. Lord, I thank you that as I draw closer to you, you open my eyes to see more and more of your presence all around me.

Thank you, Lord, that you gave me eyes to see and ears to hear so that I could proclaim your abiding presence in the world.

> Rejoice the soul of your servant, for
> to you, O Lord, I lift up my soul. (Psalm
> 86:4)

In Jesus name, Amen.

* * * * *

Lord, I pray that you will lead me to trust you with every fiber of my being. Lord, I depend on you in every situation. Lord, I trust you in every decision I make because you are leading me.

Thank you, Lord, that you hold me by your righteous right hand.

Lord, I thank you that you are always beside me and that you see everything. Lord, I pray that the light of your presence will keep me in your precious arms.

> Let the morning bring me word of your unfailing love, for I have put my trust in you. Show me the way I should go, for you. I lift up my soul. (Psalm 143:8)

In Jesus name, Amen.

* * * * *

Lord, I thank you that you lead me along the path that is uniquely right for me. I thank you that the closer I grow to you, the more fully I become who you created me to be.

Lord, I devote myself to you completely. I thank you for putting love in my heart so that I can love the Lord God with all my heart, soul, mind, and strength and love my neighbor as myself.

Lord, I rejoice in you as we journey together in intimate communion.

Thank you, Lord, for loving me and saving me, in Jesus name, Amen.

* * * * *

Lord, I thank you that you never sleep and that you watch over me while I sleep. I thank you that every morning you awaken me and open my understanding to your will. Thank you for always thinking about me.

Holy Father, straighten the tangle in my mind and enable me to see you more clearly.

Holy Spirit, lead me to spend time enjoying your presence and nourishing my soul with your Word. Open my understanding to your Word so that I can comprehend the scriptures and apply it to my life.

Lord, lead me to discern your will and empower me to handle whatever comes my way. Thank you, Lord, in Jesus name, Amen.

* * * * *

Father God, thank you that the light of your glory shines on me. Lord, I pray that the radiance of your love fall upon me and soak into the depths of my heart and mind. Lord, I want to be more like you.

Holy Father, lead me into your presence so that I can have an intimate relationship with you. Thank you, Lord, that you can use everything in my life for good.

Father God, transform me into your likeness to be more like you. Thank you, Lord, in Jesus name, Amen.

* * * * *

Loving Father, I thank you that you look at my heart. Thank you, Lord, that you work to create beauty in me to become more like you.

Holy Spirit, lead me to set aside time for nourishing my heart in the presence of God.

I pray that my heart will be guarded from evil. Thank you, Lord, that I belong to you and that your light flows through me.

Holy Spirit, lead me in the Word of God through worship and meditation.

Lord, I focus on you and remember that you are Immanuel God with us. Thank you, Lord, in Jesus name, Amen.

* * * * *

Dear Lord, I thank you for coming into this world as the light. As a child of God, I can walk in the light because you are the light and your brightness has entered into my inner being.

Holy Father, lead me to have a repenting heart so that I can walk in your ways and on the road of freedom.

Lord, as I rejoice in you, I thank you for the knowledge of your glory that shines in my heart. All glory and honor to you, O God, in Jesus name, Amen.

* * * * *

Dear Lord, I thank you that you know me and formed me in the womb.

Father God, thank you that you delight in transforming me more and more into the one you created me to be.

Thank you, Lord, that you are the skilled potter and I am the clay.

Holy Spirit, lead me to be aware of the presence of God. Thank you, Lord, that you suffered on the cross so that I will never be alone.

Thank you, Lord, that I will spend eternity with you. Thank you for guiding me through life; afterward, you will take me home to glory to be with you forever. All glory to you, Lord, in Jesus name, Amen.

* * * * *

Glorious Father, I thank you that your love chases after me every day of my life.

Heavenly Father, open the eyes of my heart to see signs of your tender presence as I go through this day.

I thank you for showing me your presence in many different ways.

Holy Father, lead me to ponder your words in my heart and give you thanks and praise for you are a great and wonderful God. Thank you for the ways you show up in my life. I pray that I will keep them in my heart and rejoice again and again that I can be strengthened. I love you, Lord, in Jesus name, Amen.

* * * * *

Father God, in the name of Jesus, I pray that you will lead me to wait on you and sit in your presence, trusting you with my whole heart.

I thank you, Lord, that it is beneficial to wait in your presence as I look up to you in hope. I acknowledge that you are in control, O Lord, and I rest in your goodness.

Thank you, Lord, for your blessings as I choose to trust you with all my heart. All praise and glory belong to you, Lord, in Jesus name, Amen.

* * * * *

Dear God, I thank you that you are taking care of me.

Holy Spirit lead me to remind myself each day that Jesus is taking care of me. I know this reminder can comfort me and help me relax.

Father God, I thank you that you know everything about me and that you watch over me. Thank you, Lord, that your resources are unlimited. I entrust everything to you, Lord, and live confidently as a child of the King of kings and Lord of lords. I rejoice in you, Lord, and thank you for being a good father, in Jesus name, Amen.

*   *   *   *   *

Dear Lord, I thank you that you are my joy, my peace, my health, my refuge, and my strength. You are everything to me, and I trust in you, O Lord. Sometimes I dwell on the past.

Holy Spirit, I need your help to forgive and let go.

Father God, turn my focus toward you and only you.

Lord, I come to you in a childlike trust. I trust you, Lord. I trust you, Lord. Thank you, Lord, for doing a new thing in my life.

Holy Father, open the eyes of my mind and heart so I can see you directing me on the way to go and how to live. Thank you, Lord, in Jesus name, Amen.

*   *   *   *   *

Father God, I thank you that you rejoice over me with singing.

Holy Spirit, lead me to open my heart, mind, and spirit to receive the richest blessings of our Lord and Savior, Jesus Christ.

Thank you, Lord, that I am your blood-bought child. Thank you that your love for me flows continuously from the throne of grace.

Lord, as I look up, I receive all that you have for me. Father God, thank you for singing songs of joy over me. Lord, as I approach you boldly with confidence, I thank you for loving me.

Holy Spirit, lead me to spend time focusing on the Lord, soaking in his presence and absorbing his Word as I set aside time to be in His presence, in Jesus name, Amen.

* * * *

Father God, I thank you for upholding me when I fall and lifting me up when I am down.

Lord, please lead me to repent and seek your presence in every situation. Thank you for your perfect love for me.

Holy Father, lead me into an intimate relationship with you. Lord, I thank you for redeeming me and turning my restlessness into calmness. Thank you, Lord, that I am called according to your purpose.

Holy Father, lead me to relax and rejoice in your steadfast love. Thank you, Lord, in Jesus name, Amen.

* * * *

Heavenly Father, I thank you for being the antidote for fear and loneliness. I thank you that you are the Lord, my God, who takes hold of me.

Father God, as I bring my feelings and everything I face in life to you, I pray that you will lead me to spend time basking in the light of your presence, realizing how safe and secure I am and that I am never alone. You, O Lord, are always with me.

Holy Father, I seek your face and your perspective on my life. Thank you for watching over me continually in the mighty name of Jesus Christ, Amen.

*   *   *   *   *

O Lord, my savior, thank you for reminding me that nothing in all creation can separate me from your love.

Holy Spirit, lead me to pause and ponder what an astonishing promise this is.

Holy Father, I thank you, and I praise you and cling to you with confidence to know that you are always with me.

Lord, I thank you that when I am feeling afraid, I can grasp your hand in a childlike trust and rest in your protection and presence and remember that perfect love drives out all fear.

Lord, your unfailing love is priceless. Hallelujah, glory be to God, in Jesus name, Amen.

*   *   *   *   *

Heavenly Father, I thank you for the strength to wake up every day striving to live more fully in your presence.

Refusing to worry about anything, Holy Spirit, lead me to pursue the Lord more and more with all my effort and energy. Not by myself, but with the leading of the Holy Spirit, I pray for help to resist the temptations of this world.

Thank you, Lord, that you are always near, ready to strengthen, encourage, and comfort me.

Holy Spirit, help me to keep my thoughts on our Savior, Jesus Christ.

Thank you, Lord, for taking great delight in me and rejoicing over me with singing, in Jesus name, Amen.

* * * *

Holy Father, I thank you as I seek your face with a smile in my heart. Thank you for your lovely presence that awaits me. Thank you that I can talk to you and bring all my concerns to you and that I can call your name, Jesus.

Holy Spirit, lead me to set my priorities according to the will of God.

Lord, I invite you into all my activities. Holy Father, I pray that you increase my joy and peace, which can only be found in you.

Lord, you are my resting place. I thank you for your everlasting hand that is always available to support me and hold me close to you, in Jesus name, Amen.

* * * *

Thank you, Lord Jesus, that you are the risen Savior. I celebrate with joy serving a Savior who is alive. Glory be to God.

Thank you, Lord, for being with me continually throughout time and eternity.

Holy Spirit, lead me to walk boldly along the path of life with our Lord and Savior.

Trusting confidently in the one who never let go of my hand, I thank you, Lord, for offering yourself so that I am forgiven for all my sins.

Holy Spirit, lead me into a heart of worshipping, singing, praising, studying, and meditating the Word of God, praying at all times, glorifying your Holy name, serving and loving others, in Jesus name, Amen.

*   *   *   *   *

Lord, I thank you that through the resurrection, I have new birth into a living hope.

I thank you for the newness of life, and I thank you that I belong to you. Thank you that the old has gone and the new has come. Thank you, Lord, that I am a new creation and that I belong to the royal family of God. Thank you, Lord, that I am changing from death to life.

I praise you, Lord, for eternal life, and I thank you that the Holy Spirit lives in me.

Holy Spirit, lead me to be transformed in my mind and put on newness of life, becoming increasingly godly, righteous, and holy.

Keep my eyes on you, O Lord, in Jesus name, Amen.

*   *   *   *   *

Lord, I rejoice that my name is written in heaven in the Book of Life, and I thank you for your promises.

Thank you for eternity, not because of my good work but because of your grace and mercy. Thank you, Lord, that I am seated with you in the heavenly realms.

I pray that I will come to you each day with open hands and a heart, saying, "Jesus, I receive your joy."

I pray that the light of your presence shines upon me and soaks into the depths of my inner being. I pray for your strength as you prepare me for the days ahead.

Lead me, O Lord, to come to you for refreshing of your spirit throughout the day, in Jesus name, Amen.

* * * * *

Heavenly Father, I thank you for your joy and peace, which are inexpressible and full of glory. Your joy and peace are great and wonderful.

Holy Father, as I come into your presence and open my heart to you, I thank you that you triumphed over sin and death.

Thank you for opening the way so that I can have a personal relationship with you for all who believe. Thank you that the salvation of my soul is secure because of the blood of Jesus Christ. Thank you that you are my Lord and Savior. I pray that your light will shine in me and that others will come to know you.

Lord, as you testify of the truth, I pray that I will join with you to walk in the truth and always wear the belt of truth, in Jesus name, Amen.

* * * * *

Father God, I thank you that your Holy hands are absolutely capable of caring for me and meeting my needs.

Holy Father, I relax in your sovereign watchful care, trusting you to do what is best, and I commit everything to you in Jesus name.

Lord, I rejoice in you that the master of time understands everything about me and loves me with an everlasting love, in Jesus name, Amen.

* * * * *

Holy Father, I come to you with thanksgiving and pray that I will draw water from the well of salvation with joy.

Knowing that you, Lord, have saved me forever from my sins and given me a spring of water that flows up in me to eternal life, I thank you and rejoice for this amazing gift and for providing for me.

Holy Father, thank you for the gift of salvation and bless me and all who are around me.

I pray that a stream of living water will flow from within me.

The Holy Spirit thinks through me, lives through me, and loves through me, in Jesus name, Amen.

*   *   *   *   *

Father God, I thank you that my steps are directed by you when the path that lies before me seems uncertain, and the best thing I can do is cling to you. Father God, I thank you that you are sovereign over my life. Father God, I thank you that I can come to you and talk to you about everything.

Holy Father, I pray that in all the choices I make, I will put you first.

Holy Spirit, lead me into an intimate relationship with our Lord and Savior, Jesus Christ, to stay in your presence and in communication with you.

I trust your guiding presence to keep me safe. Thank you, Lord, in Jesus name, Amen.

*   *   *   *   *

My sheep listen to my voice; I know
them, and they follow me. (John 10:27)

Holy Father, I thank you for this astonishingly good news for all who know you as their Savior.

Thank you for your plan and promises for my life, which are more glorious than anything I can imagine.

Holy Father, I thank you for the gift of eternity and for the light that shines on me and through me.

Lord, as I hold onto your hand in trust, dependence, and confidence that you love me and nothing will be able to separate me from your love, I enjoy the adventure of journeying with you, my savior, in Jesus name, Amen.

*   *   *   *   *

Dear Lord Jesus, I pray that the Holy Spirit of God will lead me to always be prepared to give an answer to everyone who asks me the reason for the hope I have in Jesus.

I pray that the light of Jesus will shine in me so that everyone can see you in me.

Holy Father, I pray that I will live in the awareness of your presence, trusting you fully in hope.

Holy Father, lead me to keep your Word in my heart and meditate on it daily. Thank you, Lord, in Jesus name, Amen.

*   *   *   *   *

Heavenly Father, I am willing to follow your lead, and I pray for your help.

Holy Spirit, lead me to open myself more fully to my Lord and Savior.

Holy Father, lead me to rest and relax in you as you transform me and renew my mind. Lead me to seek your face, talk to you openly, and rest in your presence.

Father God, thank you for watching over me and guiding me. Lord, I rejoice in your Holy name. Father God, I thank you that my relationship with you transcends all my circumstances.

Holy Spirit, lead me to praise you, worship you, and enjoy your presence.

Holy Father, I pray that you will increase my faith.

Holy Spirit, I pray for strength. Help me seek your face continually and fill my mind and heart with your words.

Thank you, Lord, for inner strength and peace that pass all understanding, in Jesus name, Amen.

* * * * *

Father God, I thank you that you are watching over me continually. I pray that I will seek you in every circumstance.

Lord, lead me, help me, and direct me. Lord, thank you that every breath I take depends on your sustaining power. Lord, I pray that I will rely on you in all I do and say. Thank you, Lord, for blessing me, in Jesus name, Amen.

* * * * *

Heavenly Father, I thank you that I am not my own; I was brought with a price.

Thank you, Lord, for taking all my sins and giving me your righteousness. Thank you for the invitation that calls me to come to you all who are weary and heavy burdened, and you will give them rest. Holy Father, thank you for giving me rest.

Father God, I realize that sin is terrible and burdensome, and I thank you that you have paid it in full and removed it from me forever.

Lord, I pray that every morning, I will wake up and say, "I am not my own. I belong to Jesus."

Holy Father, I pray that you will keep my feet on the path of peace. Father God, I thank you that I can find spiritual and emotional security by remembering that I belong to you and that I am your beloved.

Thank you, Father. I rejoice in you. All glory to you in Jesus name, Amen.

*   *   *   *   *

Lord, I thank you that all my trust and hope are in you, who died for me. Thank you, Lord Jesus, for leaving the glorious perfection of heaven and coming to earth to give your life for my sins so that I can have eternal life.

Thank you, Lord, that as a result of your death and resurrection, whoever believes in you will have everlasting life.

Lord, I rely on you as my savior and friend who takes care of me.

Holy Spirit, lead me to relax in the presence of Almighty God. Thank you for caring for me, O Lord, in Jesus name, Amen.

*   *   *   *   *

Heavenly Father, I thank you for your living Word, and I thank you for loving me first. Thank you for always being in me and making me spiritually alive.

Thank you, Lord, for leading me to grow more and more into the person you designed me to be. I pray that I will spend time in your tender presence.

Lord, I pray that you will lead me to delight myself in you and show kindness to others. Lord, help me to live and care for others. Thank you, Lord. In Jesus name, I pray, Amen.

* * * * *

Father God, I thank you that every day is a precious gift from you.

Lord, as I look into the day that stretches out before me, I seek your face to help me discern what is most important.

Lord, I pray that whatever I do, I will do it according to the glory of God. Show me your will and lead me to use it as a guide as I go along your pathway.

Holy Spirit, lead me to make good choices and use my time and energy to glorify God.

Holy Father, help me that when I reach the end of each day, I will be at peace about the things I have said and done. Help me, Lord, in Jesus name, Amen.

* * * * *

Heavenly Father, I thank you that I am free from fear and failure. I thank you that your love for me never fails and that when you look at me, you see me clothed in your righteousness.

Lord, I thank you for rejoicing over me with a shout of joy. Holy Father, I glorify and honor you.

Holy Spirit, work on me, changing anything that is not of you.

Thank you, Lord, for loving me and leading me to look at myself and others through the lens of your unfailing love. Father, I thank you in Jesus name, I pray, Amen.

* * * * *

Lord, I thank you for your presence. I want to enjoy your presence here and now. Lord, I invite you to be more effective in everything I engage in. I cast all anxiety and fear on you, Lord, knowing that you care for me. Open my eyes and awaken my heart so that I can fully see all the promises you have for me.

I delight in meeting with you, Lord, and thank you that you come into this world that I will have life in abundance till it overflows, in Jesus name, Amen.

* * * * *

Lord, I thank you that you know all about our troubles and that you collected all our tears and preserved them in a bottle. I thank you that I do not have to fear. Lord, I trust in you and your sovereignty. Lord, you know all about me, and you know what you are doing. O God, I pray that I will see things from your perspective.

Holy Father, I thank you that someday you will wipe away every tear from our eyes. There will be no more death, mourning, crying, or pain.

I rejoice in this glorious heavenly future awaiting us. Thank you, Lord. In Jesus name, I pray, Amen.

* * * * *

Lord, I thank you that I can come to you just as I am because you know everything about me. Thank you, Lord, that I belong to you and am loved by you. Thank you for redeeming me with your precious blood.

Holy Spirit, lead me to be honest and open to our Lord and Savior, Jesus Christ.

I come to you with humble dependence, asking that you have your way in my life, O God. Thank you that you are the potter and I am the clay. Mold me according to your will.

Lord, I lean on you, trusting you and putting all my confidence in you. Thank you for being my strength, in Jesus name, Amen.

* * * * *

Thank you, Lord, for being my father and friend and for conforming me into your likeness, which is a privilege and blessing. Thank you, Lord, for always looking out for my interests and never leaving my side. Thank you for being the friend that sticks closer than a brother.

Thank you, Lord, for your faithfulness. You are King of kings and Lord of lords, the first and last, the living one who is alive forever and ever. Thank you for being my Savior, God, and for the glorious gift of salvation.

Lead me, O Lord, to honor you with gratitude, in Jesus name, Amen.

* * * * *

Lord, I pray that you will help me not to judge on appearances and lead me to leave all judgment to you.

Holy Father, I pray that you will give me the courage to speak the truth.

Lead me, O God, to search the scriptures and my heart and ask the Holy Spirit to speak through me and love others through me. In the mighty name of Jesus, I pray, Amen.

* * * * *

Lord, I thank you that you are able to keep me from stumbling. Lord, I pray that you will hold onto me so that I will not lose my footing. Lord, I need your help, strength, and grace in making me faultless, blameless, and unblemished before the presence of the glory of God because I am clothed with the garment of salvation and the robe of righteousness.

Lord, I thank you that I am secure because it is your righteousness that saves me. Thank you for the joy that you go to prepare a place for us and will come and receive us. Wherever you are, we will be with you forever, in Jesus name, Amen.

* * * * *

Lord, when the road ahead of me seems difficult, I know I can turn to you. Lord, help me to recognize your abiding presence with me and your desire to help me. Lord, I pour out my heart to you, and I turn all my burdens to you and ask you to carry me and show me the way forward.

Lord, forgive me for wasting energy worrying about things that are beyond my control. Instead, Lord, I will use all my energy to connect to you. Lord, I seek your face continually and am ready to follow wherever you lead. I trust you, Lord, to open up the way before me as I go, in Jesus name, Amen.

* * * * *

Lord, I thank you for helping me through all the challenges in my life. Thank you, Lord, for leading me to grow stronger and more dependent on you. Lord, I thank you that you created me to live for you and walk closer to you as I journey through life.

Lord, I need your help. I trust you to lead me and that our relationship will grow stronger.

Lord, I rejoice in you, thanking you for your inner strength, in Jesus name, Amen.

* * * * *

Lord, I thank you for the sacrificial death on the cross so that everyone who calls on your name will be saved. Thank you, Lord, for saving us so that we could be part of your kingdom of everlasting life and light.

Lord, I cling to the hope I have in you. You are in control. O Lord, thank you that I can live in this world with joy and peace because you live in my heart.

Lord, as you told your disciples, so you are telling us, "Be of good cheer. You have overcome the world." In you, Lord Jesus, I find peace, in Jesus name, Amen.

* * * * *

Father God, I thank you that you are the vine and I am the branch.

Lord, I thank you that when I abide in you, you will abide in me, and we will bear much fruit. Apart from you, I cannot do anything.

Thank you, Lord, that you are alive within me and that your light flows through me. Thank you, Lord, that you chose to live inside me. Glory be to God. Thank you, Lord, for the intimacy that is so rich and for infusing me with your strength, in Jesus name, Amen.

* * * * *

Father God, I thank you joyfully for forgiving all my sins.

Lord, I thank you for your amazing promises that fill me with joy and drive out fear. Lord, thank you that my future is glorious and secure. I pray that I will have a heart of gratitude to thank you and praise you frequently.

Holy Spirit, lead me to read the Word of God and delight in your presence.

I rejoice in you, Lord, my redeemer. Thank you that nothing separates me from your love, in Jesus name, Amen.

*   *   *   *

Lord, I thank you for adopting me into the royal family. Thank you that I belong to you and that you approve of me because I am your child.

Thank you, Lord, for seeing me through the eyes of grace and for choosing me before the creation of the world to be holy and blameless in your sight.

Lord, lead me to learn to cooperate with you and embrace what you are doing in my life. Thank you for transforming me into your likeness with every increasing glory. I worship you, my father, in Jesus name. Glory be to God!

*   *   *   *

Father God, in the name of Jesus, I pray for help to fix my eyes on you. Lord, I tend to drift off on things that are not of kingdom value.

Holy Spirit, lead my mind and heart back to the Lord so that I could experience the soul-satisfying pleasures of knowing God.

Holy Spirit, lead me to seek the Lord and enjoy his presence.

Lord, you are the only one who can love me with unfailing love and give me perfect peace.

Holy Spirit, led me to fix my thoughts on the Lord Jesus Christ and rest in his presence, in Jesus name, Amen.

* * * * *

Lord, I thank you that you are my joy and strength and that your Word will sink into my heart and mind. Lord, I rest and trust in you that every day of my life will always be a good day because you are my joy and peace.

Thank you, Lord, for your unfailing love, which is priceless, and I can find refuge in the shadow of your wings no matter what is happening.

Lord, as I turn to you and drink from the river that never runs dry, I pray that you will lead me into your loving presence, in Jesus name, Amen.

* * * * *

Lord, I pour out my heart to you, knowing that you listen, you care, and that I can rely on you. You are my ever-present help in times of trouble, and I can find peace within you.

Lord, I look to you for help and guidance, and I pray that you will show me the way I should go. Lord, I turn everything over to you as I hold your hands in trust and confidence. Lord, I worship you. Lord, I rejoice in you, in Jesus name, Amen.

* * * * *

Lord, I thank you that when we have you as our savior, Lord, and friend, we have everything.

Nothing in this world can compare with the priceless treasure of eternal life, regardless of what we may lack in this world.

Lord, I am content to know that you are my savior and that I am your unique creation.

I am redeemed by your blood, Lord, as I stay in joyful communication with my Savior, who loves me more than I can imagine.

Thank you for transforming me more into the masterpiece you designed me to be, in Jesus name, Amen.

* * * * *

Lord, I thank you that your love has set me free and that the power of your love is great. Lord, I thank you that I am not my own; I was bought at a price with your holy blood. Lord, I thank you that the more I love you, the more I want to serve you with every fiber of my being. Lord, I thank you that you are perfect in all your ways. Lord, I give myself wholeheartedly to you, and I pray that you will invade the innermost core of my being.

Holy Spirit, I pray that you will take up every territory in me.

Thank you, Lord, that there is freedom in you.

In Jesus name, Amen, Amen, and Amen.

* * * * *

Lord, apart from you, I can do nothing, and you are with me and willing to help.

As I whisper, surely the Lord is in this place, and I was made to worship you, to need you, and to depend on you.

Lord, I come to you just as I am. I pray that I stay connected with you and that the Spirit will flow through me. Lord, I pray that I will live close to you and be ready to do your will, in Jesus name, Amen.

* * * * *

Lord, I thank you for continually inviting me to draw near to you.

Holy Spirit, lead me to be still in the presence of God and fix my thoughts on you.

Lord, I pray that I will relax and listen to your love whispering in my heart, and I thank you for loving me with an everlasting love.

As I meditate on the glorious truth that you are with me always, I pray that I will be aware of you as I go about my day.

Jesus, keep me aware of your presence, and I pray that these words will echo through my heart and mind frequently, in Jesus name, Amen.

* * * * *

Holy Spirit, I pray that you will lead me into stillness to sit at the feet of Jesus and listen.

Lord, I pray for an intimate connection with you and to set aside uninterrupted time to spend with you.

Holy Father, lead me to focus on the scriptures and remember that you are Immanuel God with me.

Lord, I relax in your peaceful presence as I am still and know that you are God. I pray that I will gaze on you, rejoice in your majestic splendors, and trust in your loving arms. Thank you, Lord, that you have overcome the world, in Jesus name, Amen.

* * * * *

Lord, I pray that you will lead me to walk in the light of your presence, rejoicing in your name and exalting in your righteousness. Lord, I praise you with shouts and applause. Lord, you are my savior, my shepherd, my Lord and God, and my sovereign king.

Lord, lead me to walk in your glorious light, and thank you that your blood continually cleanses me from all sins.

Holy Father, lead me to walk in your light and spend time enjoying your bright, loving presence.

In Jesus name, Amen.

* * * * *

Lord, I thank you that there is no place for pride in me for you have called me to live in joyful dependence on you.

Lord, I pray for help to live a life in obedience to you. Lord, lead me to search the scriptures and seek your face.

Holy Spirit, I pray that you will guide me along the pathway you have chosen for me. Holy Spirit, I pray that you will equip me and empower me to achieve your purpose for my life.

Thank you, Lord, that your presence is full of joy, in Jesus name, Amen.

* * * * *

Lord, I thank you and praise you for your unfailing love, which is better than life itself. Thank you, Lord, that there is no limit to your love and that it will never run out.

Your love is priceless, and I thank you that it provides a foundation for me to build on, improves my relationships with others, and helps me grow into the one you designed me to be.

Lord, I pray that I will worship you as I joyously celebrate your magnificent presence, in Jesus name, Amen.

* * * * *

Thank you, Father God, that no matter what happens in this world, I can be joyful that I am washed in the blood of Jesus.

Lord, I pray that I will remind myself every day that Jesus is with me and for me and that nothing can separate me from your love.

Holy Father, lead me to use the gift you have given me to shine the light of Jesus to others.

Lord, I pray that you will train my heart to be steadfast, trusting in you as my savior and King, in Jesus name, Amen.

* * * * *

Lord, I thank you for your loving Word that tells me not to be afraid or discouraged. Thank you, Lord, that you are always with me, holding me with your right hand, preparing me for the road ahead.

Lord, I pray that you will lead me to be still and listen to you, and I thank you for your goodness and mercy, in Jesus name, Amen.

* * * * *

Lord, as I sit quietly in your presence, lead me to remember that you are the abundance that will never run out of resources.

Your capacity to bless me is unlimited, and, Lord, thank you for the fullness of your glorious riches. Lord, thank you for your loving presence, where I have access to so much of you. As I have faith to receive, Lord, I rejoice in your abundance as I live by faith and not by sight. Thank you, Lord. In Jesus name, I pray, Amen.

* * * * *

Lord, I pray that you will lead me to come to you in every situation, and I thank you that you are my refuge and my strength. Lord, I confess all my sins to you, which you know all about before I say a word. Lord, lead me to stay in the light of your presence, receiving your forgiveness, cleansing, and healing.

Lord, thank you for clothing me in your righteousness, and nothing can separate me from your love. I thank you that whenever I stumble or fall, you are there to help me up.

Lord, as I come close to you, I pray that the light of Jesus will shine on me, in Jesus name, Amen.

* * * * *

Lord, I thank you that you are the creator of the universe. I thank you that you are with me and for me. I pray that you will lead me to connect to you on a deeper level, and I refuse to worry about anything. Thank you, Lord, that you are in charge of my life, and I pray that you will switch my focus from my problems to your presence.

> Let God have all your worries and
> cares, for he is always thinking about you
> and watching everything that concerns
> you. (1 Peter 5:7)

In Jesus name, Amen.

* * * * *

Lord, I thank you that you are sovereign over every circumstance. Lord, I come to you, humble myself under your mighty hand, and rejoice in what you are doing in my life.

Thank you, Lord, that you are the way, the truth, and the life. In you, Lord, I have everything I need both for this life and for the life yet to come.

Lord, lead me to always keep my eyes fixed on you, no matter what is going on around me. Lord, thank you that you are the center of my life, and I rejoice in you, Lord, in Jesus name, Amen.

* * * * *

Lord, as I approach this day, my desire is to serve you and honor your holy name. Lord, I thank you that before I get out of bed, you have already been working to prepare the path that will get me through the day.

Holy Spirit, lead me to search for deep treasure as I go through this day.

Thank you, Lord, that I will find you along the way.

> The Lord is my shepherd; I shall not
> want He make me lie down in green pastures. He leads me besides the still waters;

he restores my soul; he leads me in the
paths of righteousness for his name's
sake. (Psalm 23:1–3)

In Jesus name, Amen.

* * * * *

Lord, I bring my mind to you for rest and renewal, and I pray that you will infuse your presence into my thoughts.

Holy Father, I thank you for taking up residence in my heart.

I pray that my mind will stop wondering and my body will be still, relax, and regain awareness of your presence.

Thank you, Lord, that your awareness is vital to my spiritual well-being, and I thank you that my heart is your dwelling place.

Thank you, Lord, that the promise of your presence is with me at all times, and I glorify your Holy name, Amen.

* * * * *

Lord, I thank you for being with me. When I turn from my problem to your glorious presence, everything becomes lighter.

Thank you, Lord, for carrying my burden as I cast my anxiety on you. You remove it so far away that it cannot do any harm to me or anyone around me.

Lord, you delight in doing good to me because you care for me.

Shout for joy, O heavens; rejoice,
O earth; burst into song, O mountains;

for the Lord comforts his people and will
have compassion on his afflicted ones.
(Isaiah 49:13)

In Jesus name, Amen.

* * * * *

Lord, thank you that you are the one who never changes
and that you are the alpha and the omega, the first and the
last, and the beginning and the end.

Lord, only in you can I find stability; you are my peace,
my joy, and my everything.

Holy Spirit, I pray that you will lead me into the presence of God. Lord, I pray that you will redirect my thoughts
back to you as you show me the way forward.

I lift my eyes to the hills; where does
my help come from, my help comes from
the Lord, the maker of heaven and earth.
(Psalm 121:1–2)

In Jesus name, Amen.

* * * * *

Lord, I pray that your anointing be upon me, and thank
you, Lord, that you are the King of kings and Lord of lords.

Thank you that when I draw near to you, you will draw
near to me.

Thank you, Lord, that as your presence envelopes me, I
will feel overwhelmed by your power and glory. Holy Father,

lead me into a heart of worshipping you and glorifying your holy name.

Lord, lead me to enjoy the radiant beauty of your presence so that I will declare your glorious presence to others so that they will come to know you.

Thank you, Lord, in Jesus name, Amen.

* * * * *

Lord, thank you for being with me and watching over me constantly. Thank you that you are Emmanuel (God with us). Thank you that your presence enfolds me in radiant love. Thank you that nothing can separate me from your love.

Holy Spirit, I pray that you will lead me into thanksgiving, praising, and glorifying the Lord and open the door wide to your presence.

Lord, I pray that your awareness of your indwelling presence drives out discouragement and fills me with great joy.

As you, therefore, have received Christ Jesus, the Lord, so walk in him.

Thank you, Lord, in Jesus name, Amen.

* * * * *

Holy and Righteous Father, I pray that you will lead me to push back on the demands that are pressing on me. Lead me to create a safe space where I can feel your presence as I rest in you.

Holy Spirit, lead me to focus my attention on the Lord. I pray that you will strengthen me and equip me for the day ahead.

Lord, I come to you this day, and I bring you the sacrifice of my time, heart, mind, and everything else that creates sacred space around me, space that permeated with your presence and your peace.

Thank you, Lord, in Jesus name, Amen.

* * * * *

Lord, I thank you that you are involved in each moment of my life and that you carefully mapped out every inch of my journey through this day.

Lord, I trust you and know that your ways are perfect. Lord, lead me to stay conscious of you as I go through this day, remembering that you will never leave my side.

Holy Spirit, I pray that you will guide me step-by-step, protecting me and equipping me to walk in obedience to you.

Lord, I pray that the light of your presence will shine on me, giving me peace and joy.

Thank you, Lord, in Jesus name, Amen.

* * * * *

Lord, I thank you that as I relax in your healing, holy presence, I will be still as you transform my heart and mind. Lord, lead me to let go of all the cares and worries so I can receive your peace.

Thank you that you are God and that there is no one else like you.

Lord, lead me to know you intimately so that I can become more like you. Lord, I pray that you will help me to spend more time with you and relax into the comfort of your holy presence. Lord, I thank you and praise your Holy name, in Jesus name, Amen.

* * * * *

Lord, I pray that you will be the center to my entire being.

Holy Spirit, I pray that you will lead me so that my focus will always be on the Lord Jesus Christ.

I thank you, Lord, that your peace displaces fear and worries. I pray that trust and thankfulness stand guard, turning back every fear and worry before it can gain a foothold.

Lord, I thank you that there is no fear in your love, which shines on me continuously. Lead me to sit quietly in your love-light as you bless me with radiant peace, turning my whole being into trusting and glorifying you. Thank you, Lord, in Jesus name, Amen.

* * * * *

Lord, I thank you that even in challenging times, I will trust you, and I thank you that you are beside me and your spirit is within me. Lord, I thank you that the way to walk through days of challenges is to grip your precious hand tightly and stay in close communication with you.

Lord, I pray that my thoughts and spoken words are richly flavored with trust and thankfulness. Lord, I thank you that you will keep me in perfect peace as I stay close to you.

All glory and honor to you only. In Jesus name, Amen.

* * * * *

Lord, I seek your face, where I will find fulfillment in my deepest longing for the beautiful things around me. Thank you, Lord, that they are meant to be pointers to remind us of your abiding presence.

Lord, I thank you that the earth declares your glory and for pouring your light into me so that I can be a beacon to others. Lord, I pray that you will keep me from prideful ways and help me to declare your glory. Thank you, Lord, in Jesus name, Amen.

* * * * *

Lord, I thank you that I belong to you and that the light of your presence is within me. Lord, I thank you for dying for my sins. I come to you, bringing everything into the light of your love. Lord, I thank you for transforming me and cleansing me from all unrighteousness.

Lord, I thank you that you know everything about me, far more than I know about myself. I come into your presence with thanksgiving, desiring to be transformed. Thank you, Lord, in Jesus name, Amen.

* * * * *

Lord, I thank you for your love and mercy toward me. Holy Father, as I seek to live in your love, I thank you that your love covers a multitude of my sins. I pray that you will lead me to wear your love like a cloak of light covering me from head to toe.

Having no fear because perfect love drives out all fear. Lord, lead me to look at others through the lenses of love, and, Holy Spirit, lead me to be radiant with the light of your presence.

Lord, I thank you that you are my first love, and I pray that you will lead me in the splendor of holiness, in Jesus name, Amen.

* * * * *

Father God, I rest in your sovereignty, receiving each day as a gift from you.

Lord, I turn toward you, aware of your face shining upon me. Lord, I thank you for instilling joy, peace, love, and the first fruit of the Spirit in my life. Lord, I pray that you will lead me to pray continually.

Holy Spirit, I pray that you will take charge of every detail of my life, and I thank you that remembrance of you is a daily discipline.

Lord, I pray that the light of your presence be with me as I rest in you, in Jesus name, Amen.

* * * * *

Lord, I trust you and will not be afraid for you are my strength and song. Lord, I thank you that you give me power, love, and a sound mind. Lord, I trust you and sing praises to your name. Lord, I thank you that my constant need for you will create an intimate relationship with you.

Holy Spirit, I pray that you will control my mind and bless me with perfect peace and to not be conformed to this world, but be transformed by the renewing of my mind.

Thank you, Lord. In Jesus name, I pray, Amen.

* * * * *

Lord, I thank you for another day. Holy Spirit, I pray that you will help me get through this day praising and worshipping your Holy name.

Lord, I choose to walk with you along the path of peace, and I lean on you as my refuge and my strength. Lord, I thank you that you transform trials into blessings, and I cry out to you for your help.

Lord, as I turn toward you, I pray that the light of your presence shines upon me.

Thank you, Lord. In Jesus name, I pray, Amen.

* * * * *

Lord, I thank you that you are creating something new in me—a bubbling spring of joy that will spill over into the lives of others. Lord, help me not to take credit for the joy you have given me.

Lord, help me to always praise you and give you glory. Lord, lead me to watch in delight as your spirit flows through me and in me so that others will be blessed. Lord, I pray that I will become a reservoir of the fruit of the Spirit.

Holy Spirit, draw me close to you as I open up my heart to you. Holy Spirit flow in me as we walk through this day together and lead me to enjoy your presence with joy, love, and peace in Jesus name, Amen.

* * * * *

Lord, I thank you for loving me with an everlasting love. Thank you, Lord, that before the foundation of the world, you knew me and redeemed me. Lord, I thank you for revealing yourself to me, lifting me out of despair, and setting me down on a firm foundation.

Lord, I thank you for wrapping me in your robe of righteousness, and I thank you, Lord, for singing over me.

Thank you, Lord, for infusing meaning into my mind and harmony into my heart and for the light of your presence in Jesus name, Amen.

* * * * *

Lord, I thank you that you call me to walk closely with you, soaking in your presence and living in your peace.

Thank you, Lord, that before the foundation of the world, you had a plan and made promises for my life. I thank you that I am a child of God, and I thank you that you require of me to act justly, to love, and to walk humbly with you wherever you lead.

> For I know the plans I have for you,
> declare the Lord. Plans to prosper you
> and not harm you. Plan to give you hope
> and a future. (Jeremiah 29:11)

In Jesus name, Amen.

* * * * *

Lord, I thank you for your words that tell me, "My peace I leave with you, and my peace I give unto you. Let your heart not be troubled or afraid." Lord, as I relax and know that you are God, you are my refuge and strength.

Holy Spirit, I pray that you will lead me to learn to laugh as my heart is lifted into heavenly places and the melodies of praise go up to you.

Lord, lead me to desire your will above all else. I pray that you will lead me to enjoy the joy of your presence. Holy Spirit think, live, and love through me.

Thank you, Lord, in Jesus name, Amen.

* * * * *

Lord, I thank you that you speak to me continually and that your nature is to communicate with me. Lord, I thank you for your loving Word, and I thank you for the beauty of your creation. Lord, I thank you that you speak in the depths of my spirit, where you take up residence.

Holy Spirit, I pray that you will sharpen my spiritual eyes and ears.

Lord, I thank you for your presence and that I will seek you and find you when I seek you with all my heart. Thank you, Lord, in Jesus name, Amen.

* * * * *

Lord, I come to you with thanksgiving. I pray that you will lead me to be thankful at all times. Lord, I thank you that my thankfulness awakens me to rest in your presence.

Let us fix our eyes on Jesus, the author and finisher of our faith, who, for the joy set before him, endured the cross. Scorning its shame, he sat down at the right hand of the throne of God.

Lord, I thank you in Jesus name, Amen.

* * * * *

Lord, I open my hands and heart to receive this day as a precious gift from you. Lord, thank you for this new day that announces your radiant presence and for preparing the way before me.

Holy Spirit, I pray that as soon as I wake up every morning, there will be praise, worship, and thanksgiving to you Lord.

Thank you that you are God, from whom all blessings flow and who create all wondrous work. Thank you, Lord, for taking great delight in me and rejoicing over me with singing.

Glory be to your Holy name. Thank you, Lord, in Jesus name, Amen.

* * * * *

Mighty God, I pray that you will help me to stay conscious of your presence.

Lord, I thank you that you go before me as well as with me throughout each day.

Thank you, Lord, that nothing take you by surprise. I thank you that no circumstance can overwhelmed me because you are with me.

Lord, I look to you as the source of my life. You are my everything, and I fix my eyes on you and bring every thought captive to you.

Lord, I bring my restless heart to you and wait as you speak peace into the depths of my soul. Thank you, Lord, in Jesus name, Amen.

* * * * *

Lord, I pray that you will lead me to rest in your Holy Spirit. I pray that I will focus all my attention on you as you are my constant companion.

Lord, I trust that you will equip me fully for the journey that I should take. Thank you, Lord, that you are my protector. Lord, I thank you for meeting me in this present moment. Lord, as I refresh in your presence and breathe deeply, knowing that every breath I take belongs to you, Lord, I enjoy your presence, knowing that you are with me and watching over me. Thank you, Lord, in Jesus name, Amen.

*   *   *   *   *

Lord, I thank you that I can taste and see that you are good. I thank you that this command contains an invitation to experience your living presence and your promises.

Lord, I thank you that the more I experience you, the more convinced I become of your goodness. I thank you for this knowledge, which is essential to my faith and walk with you.

Holy Spirit, lead me to spend time enjoying and experiencing the goodness of the Lord.

> For my thoughts are not your thoughts, nor are your ways my ways, says the Lord.
>
> For as the heavens are higher than the earth, so are my ways higher than your ways.
>
> And my thoughts are better than your thoughts. (Isaiah 55:8–9)

In Jesus name, Amen.

*   *   *   *   *

Lord, I thank you that you are the truth, who come to set me free.

Thank you, Holy Spirit, for controlling my mind and actions more fully as I become free in you. Thank you, Lord, as the Holy Spirit works in me. I am becoming more like you every day.

Holy Spirit, lead me to yield to the spirit as I sit in the stillness of your presence and focus my entire being on you.

Lord, I thank you that you are the way, the truth, and the life. Lord, thank you for leading me along the paths of newness.

Lord, thank you that my security comes from knowing the one who died to set me free, in Jesus name, Amen.

* * * * *

Lord, I pray that you will lead me to know your ways, and I thank you for guiding me continually so I can relax and enjoy your presence.

Holy Spirit, lead me to discipline my thoughts and trust your work in my life. Lead me to pray about everything and leave the outcome to you.

Lord, I thank you for guiding me with your counsel. Lord, I bring all my concerns to you, in Jesus name, Amen.

* * * * *

Father God, I pray that you will forgive me for judging others. Thank you, Lord, that you are the only capable judge and that you have acquitted me through your precious blood. Your acquittal came as a price for your sacrifice on the cross.

Lord, I pray that you will lead me to live close to you and absorb your Word. Holy Spirit, please guide me, lead me, and correct me.

Thank you, Lord, that there is no condemnation for those who belong to Christ Jesus. I rejoice in you always, O God, in Jesus name, Amen.

* * * * *

Lord, I worship you in spirit and in truth, as I join with the choir of angels who are continually before the throne, Holy, Holy, Holy, Lord God Almighty.

Lord, I thank you that my praise and thanksgiving are heard in heaven, and I thank you that petitions are also heard.

Lord, I pray that I will have a heart of gratitude that clears the way to my heart. Thank you that your blessings have fallen upon me in rich abundance.

Lord, I thank you for your blessing of nearness to you, which gives me abundant joy and peace. Lord, lead me to practice praise and thanksgiving continually.

In Jesus name, Amen.

* * * * *

Lord, as I draw near to you with a thankful heart, I am aware that my cup is overflowing with blessings. Lord, I thank you that gratitude enables me to perceive you more clearly and rejoice in our love relationship.

Thank you, Lord, for your Word that tells me nothing can separate me from your loving presence. Lord, I thank you that every day I get up. I will remind myself that my security rests in you alone and that you're totally trustworthy.

Lord, I thank you for the glorious adventure you have planned for me. Holy Spirit, please keep me away from my old ways.

Thank you, Lord, for doing something new within me. Lead me to be on the lookout for all that you have prepared for me. Lord, I rejoice in your holy name, in Jesus name, Amen.

* * * * *

Father God, I thank you that I am a child of the everlasting King. Lord, I thank you for this new day.

Holy Spirit, lead me to push back everything and make room for the Lord, and sit still in his presence.

Lord, I seek your face. Holy Spirit, I pray for help to control my mind. Lead me to be still and attentive in your presence.

Thank you, Lord, that as I sit in your presence, I am on Holy ground, and, Lord, I recognize my dependence on you and you alone.

Glory to your Holy name, in Jesus name, Amen.

* * * * *

Lord, I thank you that I can trust you in all my thoughts.

Thank you, Holy Spirit, for helping me to direct my thoughts toward you.

I thank you, Lord, for leading me to practice thinking the way that pleases you, trusting you, praising you, and thanking you as those thoughts become more like yours.

I reject negative and sinful thoughts in Jesus name. I confess every sin I committed, and I pray, Lord, that you will forgive me.

Thank you, Lord, for keeping my mind in your presence and my feet on the path of peace, in Jesus name, I pray, Amen.

* * * * *

Lord, I thank you that as I seek your face, I pray that every thought will be holy and righteous. Lord, I thank you for loving me. Thank you that you are God of unlimited abundance. Holy Spirit, lead me to open wide my heart and mind to receive more and more of you.

> We fix our eyes not on what is seen
> but on what is unseen. For what is seen is
> temporary, but what is unseen is eternal.
> (2 Corinthians 4:18)

Thank you, Lord, in Jesus name, Amen.

* * * * *

Heavenly Father, I thank you for this new day.

Holy Spirit, I call upon you for help, and I pray that you will quiet my mind to think godly thoughts. Thank you, Lord, for speaking softly into the depths of my being. When my mind wonders, Holy Spirit, help me to bring my thoughts back to you.

Thank you, Lord, that I am transformed by the renewing of my mind. Lord, lead me to sit quietly in your presence as you reprogram my thinking. Thank you, Lord, for renewing my mind, in Jesus name, Amen.

* * * * *

Lord, I pray that you will lead me to relax in your peaceful presence.

Holy Spirit, lead me into the sacred space of communion with our Lord and Savior, Jesus Christ.

Thank you, Lord, for your desire to have an intimate relationship with me.

Lord, I pray that you will lead me to trust you with all my heart, soul, mind, and strength. Lord, I surrender everything to your precious hands. You give us eternal life, and we shall never perish. No one can snatch us out of your hand, in Jesus name, Amen.

*　*　*　*

Lord, I worship you, I praise you, and I glorify your holy name. Lord, I seek you as I experience your joy and peace. Lord, I thank you that the light of your presence is brilliant and everlasting. Lord, I pray that you will lead me to walk in your light and that I will become a beacon through whom others will draw and see the light of Jesus in me.

> Therefore, let everyone who is Godly pray to you while you may be found. Surely, when the mighty waters rise, they will not reach him. (Psalm 32:6)

Thank you, Lord, in Jesus name, Amen.

*　*　*　*

Lord, I pray that you will remind me, whenever I feel distant from you, to whisper your Holy name.

Jesus, Jesus, I trust you and I thank you that when I call your name in prayer, it restores awareness of your presence. Father, I pray that you forgive me for using your name in vain. Your name is precious, loving, and true. Help me to whisper your name and stay in your presence.

Thank you, Lord, for calling me to yourself in the most personal way. Thank you, Jesus, that you have inscribed me on the palm of your hand; your walls are continually before me.

Thank you, Lord, in Jesus name, Amen.

* * * * *

Lord, I thank you that you called me to experience the riches of your salvation which brings me joy.

Lord, I thank you that I am your beloved child.

Holy Spirit, I pray that you will lead me to fix my eyes on you, the lover of my soul.

Lord, I pray that you will lead me to praise you and glorify your Holy name.

Thank you, Lord, for seeing me dressed in righteousness and radiance in your perfect love. Thank you, Lord, for being my intercessor, my protector, and my everything. Thank you, Lord, that you understand me completely, in Jesus name, Amen.

* * * * *

Lord, I pray that you will keep me walking along the path you have chosen for me. Lord, I pray that you will lead me to take the next step while I cling to your hand for strength and direction.

Holy Spirit, lead me to stay on the path that you have selected for me. Holy Spirit, I pray that you will think through me, listen through me, and love through me.

Holy Spirit, thank you for the word of wisdom to share the Gospel of Jesus Christ. Lead me to direct every person toward our savior.

Thank you, Lord, for your faithfulness, in Jesus name, Amen.

* * * * *

Lord, I thank you that you tell us not to worry about tomorrow, and I thank you that it is not a suggestion but a command. Lord, I thank you that your grace is sufficient for me. Lord, I trust you in every area of my life, and I thank you that trusting you brings me directly into your presence. Lord, I thank you for allowing me to enjoy your presence continually by trusting you at all times. Blessed are the poor in spirit for there is the kingdom of God.

Thank you, Lord. In Jesus name, I pray, Amen.

* * * * *

Lord, I thank you that when I am feeling despair, I can look to you. Lord, I thank you that I can look up and see the light of your presence shining down on me. Lord, I thank you that as I focus on you in trust, I will rise above every despair.

Lord, as I hold your hand, I pray that you will put a firm grip on me. Lord, I thank you for pulling me out of darkness into your marvelous light, and I pray that you cleanse me of everything that does not line up with your Word.

Thank you, Lord, for covering me with your righteousness and walking with me down the path of light. Thank you, Lord, in Jesus name, Amen.

* * * * *

Lord, I thank you that you are near me and that your rich presence is present in every moment.

Holy Spirit, open my eyes so that everywhere and in everything I will see the hands of the Lord in my life. Thank you, Lord, that the more aware I am of your presence, the safer I feel.

Lord, I thank you that you are real and that I can hear you, see you, and touch you.

Glory be to God.

> Now faith is the substance of things hoped for, the evidence of things not seen. (Hebrews 11:1)

I trust you, Lord, in Jesus name, Amen.

* * * * *

Lord, I thank you that when I seek your face, I will find all that I long for, the deepest longing of my heart for more intimacy with you.

Lord, I thank you that you designed me to desire you and pray that you will lead me into the stillness of your presence. Lord, I thank you that I will follow you more closely, leading more fully, so that I can develop the gift to follow you wholeheartedly.

Lord, I thank you that when I draw near to you, you will draw near to me, and others will be blessed. Lord, I thank you for the light of your presence that shines upon me, in Jesus name, Amen.

* * * * *

Lord, I pray that you will lead me to rest in your presence.

Lord, I need a refreshing of your Holy Spirit. Lord, I thank you that when I relax in your presence, I will cry out to you. I trust you and thank you for your Word.

> For thus says the Lord God, the Holy one of Israel: In returning and resting, you shall be saved. In quietness and confidence shall be your strength. (Isaiah 30:15)

Thank you, Lord. In Jesus name, I pray, Amen.

* * * * *

Lord, I thank you that there is freedom in you. Thank you, Lord, that you are my master, my father, and my everything. Lord, I pray that I will concentrate on staying close to you at all times.

Lord, I thank you that you came to set me free. You shall know the truth, and the truth shall make you free. Thank you, Lord. In Jesus name, I pray, Amen.

* * * * *

Lord, I thank you that I can relax in your presence as you lead me throughout this day and always. Lord, I pray that you will direct every step I take. And I thank you for directing me and setting me free so that I can enjoy your presence.

Lord, as I walk with you along the path of life, I pray that the light of Jesus will shine on me, brightly lighting up my life so that others will see Jesus in me. Thank you, Lord, in Jesus name, Amen.

* * * * *

Lord, I thank you that your love seeps into the inner part of my being. Lord, I open up to you and repent of all my sins. Thank you, Lord, that you know everything about me.

Lord, I open myself fully to your transforming presence. I pray that your love and light search out and destroy hidden fear.

Holy Spirit, lead me to spend time with you as your love soaks into my innermost being. Lord, lead me to enjoy your perfect love, which expels every trace of fear. Thank you, Lord, for forgiving me of all my sins, in Jesus name, Amen.

* * * * *

Lord, lead me to come to you continually being thankful that you are the anchor of my soul.

Holy Spirit, please lead me and help me not to drift. Holy Spirit, pull me back into your presence and lead me to always feel that inner tug telling me to return to your presence.

> My sheep hear my voice, and I
> know them, and they follow me.

> And I give unto them eternal life;
> and they shall never perish, neither shall
> any man pluck them out of my hand.
> (John 10:27–28)

Thank you, Lord, in Jesus name, Amen.

* * * * *

Lord, I pray that you will lead me to trust you in the depths of my being and lead me to live in constant communication with you. Lord, I thank you that you are with me and within me.

Thank you, Lord, that you do not condemn me. Thank you for encouraging me and supporting me, and I pray that you will quiet my mind in your presence so that I can hear you.

Thank you for the peace that you have given me.

> The Lord bless you and keep you.
> The Lord will make his face shine
> upon you and be gracious to you.
> The Lord turned his face towards
> you and gave you peace. (Numbers
> 6:24–26)

In Jesus name, Amen.

* * * * *

Lord, as I come to you today, I bring you the sacrifice of my time, my life, and everything else.

Holy Spirit, I pray that you will lead me to sit quietly in your presence.

Lord, I thank you for your blessings that flow like streams of living water. Thank you, Lord, that you are the one from whom all blessings flow, and I am blessed by our time together.

Lord, I pray that you will lead me to glorify you as I delight in you. Lord, I love your presence. I enjoy your presence now and forever. Thank you, Lord, in Jesus name, Amen.

* * * * *

Lord, I pray that I will sit quietly in your presence. Thank you for loving me and blessing me. Lord, lead me to soak in your presence and lead me to keep looking to you and communicating with you as we walk through this day together.

Lord, lead me to fill my mind with your words. I pour out my heart to you. Thank you, Lord, that you are my refuge and my strength. Trust in him at all times, O people, and pour out your hearts to him for God is our refuge. Thank you, Lord, in Jesus name, Amen.

* * * * *

Father God, I thank you that in every situation, I will trust you. Lord, I bring everything to you and leave it in your capable hands.

Lord, lead me to stay in touch with you through thankful, trusting prayers and rest in your sovereign control.

> Lord, I rejoice in you and exult in the
> God of your salvation. (Habakkuk 3:18)

> This is the message we have heard
> from him and declare to you: God is
> light; in him there is no darkness at all.
> (1 John 1:5)

When I am afraid, I put my trust in you. Thank you, Lord, in Jesus name, Amen.

* * * * *

Lord, I thank you that you speak to me, and I hear you in the depths of my heart. Deep call unto deep thank you, Lord, for the blessing to hear you directly.

Lord, help me to never take this blessing for granted and help me to respond with a heart overflowing with gratitude. Holy Spirit, I pray that you will lead me to cultivate a thankful mindset.

Lord, I pray that you will lead me to a heart of joy.

> You guide me with your counsel,
> and afterward you receive me to glory.
> (Psalm 73:24)

In Jesus name, Amen.

* * * * *

Lord, I thank you for your robe of righteousness and for covering me from head to toe. I thank you, Lord, for the blood that was paid in full.

Thank you, Lord, for the gift of righteousness. Holy Spirit, lead me to keep my eyes on you as I practice walking in the garment of salvation.

Holy Spirit, lead me to throw off the unrighteous behavior so that I may feel at ease in your glorious garment. Lord, lead me to enjoy the gift you fashioned for me before the foundation of the world.

Glory be to God. Thank you, Lord, in Jesus name, Amen.

* * * * *

Lord, I thank you for this day and for leading me to relax in your healing, holy presence. Lord, I pray that you will transform me as I spend this time alone with you. Lord, I pray that my thoughts will center more and more on you and that trust will replace worry and fear. Lord, lead me to spend time with you as my trust in you increases. Lord, lead me to focus on what is important as I walk close to you.

Holy Spirit, saturate my mind with your Word.

> Your word is a lamp to my feet and
> a light to my path. (Psalm 119:105)

Thank you, Lord, in Jesus name, Amen.

* * * * *

Lord, I thank you for inviting me to come to you. I pray that you will quiet my heart and mind so that I can hear you.

Lord, you tell me if I draw near to you, you will draw near to me as I open myself to your loving presence.

I pray that you may fill me with your fullness so that I can experience how wide, how long, how high, and how deep your love is for me.

Thank you, Lord, for your love that surpasses all understanding. Submit yourselves then to God. Resist the devil, and he will flee from you. Draw near to God, and he will draw near to you. Thank you, Lord, in Jesus name, Amen.

* * * * *

Lord, I thank you for calling me to come to you when I am feeling weak and weary and rest in your everlasting arms.

Lord, I thank you that you are my strength. When I am weak, I am strong because you uphold me with your righteous hand. Lord, thank you for your gift that provides opportunities for my spirit to blossom in your presence. Lord, I accept the gift you have given me. Lead me to use it for your glory. I pray that you will bless me richly through it.

The Lord has appeared of old to me, saying, "Yes, I have loved you with an everlasting love." Therefore, with loving-kindness, I have drawn you.

Thank you, Lord, in Jesus name, Amen.

* * * * *

Lord, I pray that you will lead me to meet you in the early morning. I thank you that you eagerly await me in the stillness of your holy presence.

Lord, I thank you for renewing my strength and saturating me with peace.

Holy Spirit, lead me to commune with the creator of the universe. Holy Spirit, I pray that you will awaken in my heart a strong desire to know you more.

Lord, I seek your face to hear your love call for my life. Lord, I delight in everything that is true, noble, pure, lovely, and admirable.

Lord, I pray that the light of Jesus will shine in me day by day, in Jesus name, Amen.

* * * * *

Lord, I thank you that I can call upon the name that is above all other names: Jesus, Jesus, Jesus. Lord, I thank you that you are with me and that you will never leave me or forsake me.

Lord, I thank you that I find strength and peace through praying in your name. Lord, I pray that you will lead me to yield to your design and purpose for my life.

Thank you that nothing can separate me from your loving presence, and I belong to you, in Jesus name, Amen.

* * * * *

Lord, I thank you and praise your Holy name. I thank you that you infused your light into me, empowering me to depend on you and to live in your presence.

Lord, lead me so that in every situation, I will cry out to you and allow you to fight for me. Lord, I thank you for working on my behalf as I rest in the shadow of your almighty presence.

Lord, I thank you that you are the living Word as I bask in the beauty of your presence. Lord, lead me to praise you, worship you, and give glory to your Holy name.

> In the beginning was the Word, and
> the Word was with God, and the Word
> was God. (John 1:1)

In Jesus name, Amen.

* * * * *

Lord, I thank you for healing all my brokenness. I thank you that your very presence has immerse healing powers.

Lord, I pray that you will lead me to live in your presence and grow more and more into an intimate relationship with you.

Lord, I thank you that you are with me, within me, and all around me.

> Now to him who is able to do
> exceedingly abundantly above all that we
> ask or think according to the power that
> works in us. (Ephesians 3:20)

Thank you, Lord. In Jesus name, I pray, Amen.

* * * * *

Lord, I thank you that you have chosen the path for me to take, and I pray that you will lead me in your presence.

Lord, I pray that I will experience your glorious presence and tell others about your loving-kindness. Lord, I thank you for the work that you are doing in me so that it will blossom and burst forth, and abundant fruit will be born.

Lead me to stay on the path of life with you, trusting you wholeheartedly. Holy Spirit, I pray that you will fill me with joy and peace.

Thank you, Lord, in Jesus name, Amen.

* * * * *

Lord, I thank you that you call me to trust you and not be afraid.

Holy Spirit, help me so that when I start to be afraid, you lead me to affirm my trust in you. Lord, I thank you that in every circumstance, I can call your name, Jesus, Jesus, Jesus.

Lord, lead me to refresh myself in your Holy presence and lead me to speak and sing praises to your Holy name.

As your face shines radiantly upon me, thank you, Lord, that there is no condemnation for those who belong to you.

Thank you that you are my strength, song, and salvation, in Jesus name, Amen.

* * * * *

Lord, I entrust my love to you and release everything into your hands. Holy Spirit, I pray that you lead me away from idols and give me strength to keep my heart on you.

Lord, I thank you for your presence that go with me, and give me rest.

Lord, as I relax and place my trust in you, I thank you that you watch over me.

> You are my hiding place; you will
> protect me from trouble and surround me
> with songs of deliverance. (Psalm 32:7)

Thank you, Lord, in Jesus name, Amen.

* * * * *

Lord, I thank you that you are all around me and hovering over me as I seek your face. Lord, I thank you that you are near to me, closer than the air I breathe.

Holy Spirit, lead me to recognize the presence of God. Lord, I thank you that in your presence, I am never alone.

Thank you, Lord, that you know everything about me. Thank you, Lord, that I have nothing to fear for I am being cleansed by the blood of Jesus Christ and clothed in his righteousness.

Thank you, Lord, for living in me and for your intimacy of nearness, in Jesus name, Amen.

* * * * *

Loving Father, I come to you in the mighty name of Jesus with all my fears and weaknesses out in the open. I lay down the masks that I hide behind and open my heart to you. Give me the courage to trust you.

Lord, I want to do your will—what honors you, what pleases you. Holy Spirit, I need your help. In Jesus name, I pray, Amen.

* * * * *

Father God, I pray that you will help me win the battle in my mind. Thank you that I have a mind for Christ.

Lord, I trust you that I will go in the direction of your Word and that you will be my strength and my high tower.

Spirit of Almighty God touch me, fill this vessel with oil that there be light in me.

In Matthew 5:14, Father God, you tell me, "I am the light of the world; a city that is set on a hill cannot be hidden." You tell me in 2 Timothy 1:7, "For God has not given us a spirit of fear but of power, love, and a sound mind."

I believe in my heart the words that you spoke to me, and I pray for those who do not know you.

Father God, I pray for forgiveness for all our sins. Thank you for sending your son to die on the Calvary Cross to redeem us from sin.

Thank you that all your promises are yes and amen, in Jesus name, Amen.

* * * * *

For he himself is our peace, who
has made both one and has broken down
the middle wall of separation. (Ephesians
2:14)

Father God, thank you that you are my joy and peace. Thank you for breaking down the middle wall of separation. I can come straight to you in the Holy of Holies.

Father God, turn my heart to your desire. Help me to cooperate with the work that you called me to do. Help me to be sensitive to the Holy Spirit. Father God, help me to be more like you every day. In Jesus name, I pray, Amen.

* * * * *

That the God of our Lord Jesus
Christ, the father of glory, may give unto

me the spirit of wisdom and revelation in
the knowledge of him. (Ephesians 1:17)

Lord, I worship you as the unique Word of God. I pray today for fresh revelation of who you are and a deeper understanding of what it means to be called a child of God.

Lord, today I want to seek you and thank you that you have revealed yourself in Jesus Christ, full of grace and truth. Help me to live a life that is full of grace and truth.

I call on you for help in all the tasks I undertake and all the words that I speak, in Jesus name, Amen.

* * * * *

Heavenly Father, open the eyes of my heart as in Ephesians 1:18. The eyes of my understanding are being enlightened so that I may know the hope of your calling.

What are the riches of the glory of His inheritance in the saints.

Bless the Lord, my soul, and all that
is within me.
Bless his holy name.
Bless the Lord, O my soul, and
do not forget all his benefits. (Psalm
103:1–2)

I say to my soul: "Soul bless the Lord at all times." Always praise the Lord. Always worship the Lord. Always give thanks to the Lord, in Jesus name, Amen.

* * * * *

> On the last day, that great day of the
> feast, Jesus stood and cried out, "If any-
> one thirsts, let him come to me and drink.
> He who believes in me, as the scripture
> has said, out of his heart will flow rivers
> of living water." (John 7:37–38)

Father God, your desire for us is to take you in, to drink of you as the living water. Lord, in the scripture, you stood up and cried out, issuing a call for us to come to you and drink. Only you, Lord Jesus, can quench my inner thirst. I come to you, Father, and I thank you that as I drink of you, out of my heart will flow rivers of living water.

Father God, with joy, I will draw water from the wells of salvation. Jehovah God, I give you thanks. Thank you for sending your son through his death and resurrection we are saved. Thank you for caring for our needs. Thank you for family, food, home, health, and life.

Father God, I pray that I will always give thanks to you. As I give thanks, I continue to drink the living water that refreshes me each day, in the name of Jesus, Amen.

* * * * *

Heavenly Father, deep down in my heart, I know I must trust your guidance and not the way of the world. Please give me a heart of discernment. May I listen to wise and godly counsel and not bad advice.

Holy Spirit, lead me to stand bold in my faith and meditate on your powerful word from Isaiah 30:21: "Your ears shall hear a word behind you, saying, 'This is the way; walk in it.' Whenever you turn to the right or whenever you turn to the left."

Help me, Father God, to meditate on your Word and trust in it, in Jesus name, Amen.

* * * * *

Father God, I praise you and glorify you. I worship you and honor you. Father God, I thank you for the covenant that you make with us. Thank you for putting your laws into our hearts and writing them in our minds.

Thank you that our sins and lawless deeds you remember no longer. Thank you for your death and resurrection so that we can enter the Holiest of Holiest with boldness by the blood of Jesus Christ.

Thank you for the new and living way that you consecrated for us through the veil that is the flesh of Jesus Christ.

Thank you, Lord, for being our high priest. I pray that you will draw us to you with a true heart, in Jesus name, Amen.

* * * * *

Good morning, Father God, in the name of Jesus, my Savior and King, I present myself to you. I lay my wills, my ways, and my everything at the altar before you. Use me for your glory and the good of your people. In full trust and worship, I commit myself to obeying you (Read Romans 12).

Father God, thank you that you know what's best for me, your daughter.

Father God, thank you as you feed me with your living Word. I am transform day by day in my mind, and my heart is changing as I submit to my Lord and Savior, Jesus Christ. I depend upon you, observe your commands, and trust you to mold me to please you.

You are awesome, God.

Holy Spirit, lead me to live in the center of the will of God.

Father God, thank you that we are buried with you in baptism and raised with you to walk in the newness of life.

Thank you for the death and resurrection of Jesus Christ, which gave us a new nature and the power to live for God.

Thank you that the resurrection of Christ is in us.

Thank you, Father God, that death has been defeated, and we walk in obedience to our Lord and Savior, Jesus Christ.

> The wages of sin is death, but the
> gift of God is eternal life in Jesus Christ,
> our Lord. (Romans 6:23)

Father God, thank you that you are our only hope. Thank you for sending your son, Jesus. Thank you for the free gift that Jesus Christ purchased for us on the cross. Thank you, Lord. I worship you. I glorify you, and I rejoice in you. All glory and honor to you, my father. In Jesus name, I pray, Amen.

* * * * *

Father God, I thank you that I am created in your image. I thank you that the Holy Spirit will lead me and that my personality will reflect you.

Holy Spirit, help me to keep my tongue from evil. Help me to uplift others and be kind.

Father God, help me to have a heart that forgives.

Holy Spirit, help me to think about the promises of God and allow them to fill my heart and mind with peace.

Father God, lead me to always remember that I belong to you and that I am a child of God.

O Father, let the beauty of Jesus show through me each day.

> Let the words of my mouth and
> the meditation of my heart be acceptable
> in your sight, O Lord, my strength and
> redeemer. (Psalm 19:14)

Heavenly Father, lead me to be gentle and loving to those with whom I come into contact.

Lead me, O God, to be the salt of the earth that Jesus called us to be.

Holy Father, I pray that people will see the beauty of Christ in me and come to know our Lord and Savior, Jesus Christ. May I say and do only what brings glory to your name, in the name of Jesus, our Lord, Amen.

* * * * *

> This book of the law shall not depart
> from your mouth, but you shall meditate
> on it day and night that you may observe
> according to all that is written in it.
> For then you shall make your way
> prosperous, and then you shall have good
> success. (Joshua 1:8)

Dear Lord, please help me to cherish your words by speaking them, meditating on them, and obeying them. In doing so, I ask that you bless me as only you can.

Father, I pray that I will apply your Word to every aspect of my life, in Jesus name, I pray, Hallelujah, Amen.

* * * * *

Good morning, Father God. I place this day in your hands. I thank you, praise you, and glorify you. You are a great and mighty King. Thank you for your faithfulness; you have been so good to me.

I pray that you will prune me and remove anything that hinders me from fully focusing on and serving you. Remove anything that is blocking me from having a closer relationship with you. Take away those things that are distractions: idols, unforgiveness, hate, and pride. Give me the strength to remove everything from my life that is not pleasing to you. Holy Spirit, lead me and help me.

I want to be more and more like you, Lord Jesus.

I pray that I will always walk in the light and always please you.

> Your word is a lamp to my feet and
> a light to my path. (Psalm 119:105)

Father, help me to keep your Word in my heart. Give me grace to put you first as my number one priority. I will forever place you above all things.

Holy Spirit, lead me to love the Lord with all my heart, soul, mind, and strength.

> And do not be conformed to this
> world, but be transformed by the renew-
> ing of your mind, that you may prove
> what is that good, acceptable, and perfect
> will of God. (Romans 12:2)

Holy Spirit, do a transformation in me. Transform my mind and transform my way of thinking. Give me the desire to hunger and thirst after you. I pray for a heart of worship, so I will worship you in spirit and truth.

Holy Righteous Father, I pray all these things in Jesus name, my Lord and Savior, Hallelujah, Amen.

* * * * *

Father God, I thank you that before the foundation of the world, you promised to redeem your children by sending Jesus Christ the Messiah.

> I am not ashamed of the gospel
> of Christ, for it is the power of God to
> bring salvation to everyone who believes,
> for the Jew first and for the Greek also.
> (Romans 1:16)

Our Heavenly Father, thank you for the free gift of salvation that you have given us. Holy Spirit lead me to represent our Lord and Savior with boldness.

> For in it the righteousness of God is
> revealed from faith to faith, as it is writ-
> ten, The just shall live by faith. (Romans
> 1:17)

Father God, thank you that we live our whole lives by faith in Jesus Christ. Thank you for teaching me, empowering me, and equipping me, Lord. Help me to grow in godliness by trusting you. Teach me to submit myself in full obedience to you so that your name will be glorified.

Thank you, Father God, that your desire for me is to know you more. Thank you for providing a way for us to have a relationship with you through Jesus Christ. I praise you, I glorify you, and I honor you. Holy Father, I rejoice in you. In Jesus name, I pray, Amen.

* * * * *

Read Romans 1.

Father, I come to you to renounce other masters and identify myself with Jesus as I discover His will and live according to his Word. I pray that I will turn from all conflicting interests and keep my focus on you, Heavenly Father.

Father God, thank you for sending your son, Jesus Christ, who died and was raised from the dead. That opens the door for God's grace and kindness to pour on us.

Father God, thank you that you call me to witness to others.

Holy Spirit lead me in obedience.

Thank you, Father God, that because of Jesus Christ, we have become a part of God's family and are his very own holy people. Set apart for his service, Holy Spirit lead me to share the love of Jesus with others.

Father God, rekindle a fire in me that I will follow you and tell others about this amazing news that has the power to change people's lives for eternity, in Jesus name, Amen.

* * * * *

Be still and know that I am God. I
will be exalted among the nations, and I
will be exalted in the earth. (Psalm 46:10)

Father God, I pray for stillness so that I will sit at your feet and listen to you as Mary did.

And she had a sister called Mary,
who also sat at Jesus' feet and heard his
word. (Luke 10:39)

Father, I pray that my life will be centered around the good portion, as Mary chose the good portion. I want all my days to be marked by choosing to sit at the feet of Jesus.

Lord, I sought to have a relationship with you above all else.

Father God, I thank you for the Holy Spirit, and I pray that you will fill every space in me with your nearest. Heavenly Father, thank you for having the power to satisfy my longing soul.

Father God, lead me to cast aside all other concerns and to center my life around abiding by you. Lord, may my will be filled with remarkable, heavenly, and eternal impact.

Father, I pray this in the name of Jesus Christ, Amen.

* * * * *

Father God, my desire is to share in the secret of your promise. Thank you for your promise of yes and amen.

I want to know your heart. Purify me, Lord, and let my lifestyle reflect you so that I can have an intimate relationship with you.

Lord, I want to abide in your presence so that every-thing I do will honor and glorify you. Lord, I want to feel your presence. Lord, I want to hear you talk to me.

Breathe on me, Holy Father. Touch me, Holy Father.

Thank you for never leaving me or forsaking me. Thank you for being a good father to me. I rejoice in you and glorify you. I honor you, Father. In Jesus name, I pray, Amen.

*   *   *   *   *

Father God, help me to devote myself to praying with an alert mind and a thankful heart. Help me to stay con-nected to you in everything I do.

Holy Spirit, help me to call on you even when I engage in other activities. I invite you to everything I do so that my work will be better and my life will be more fulfilling. Help me set a time to communicate with you.

Holy Spirit, you are my helper. Empower my prayer life.

Heavenly Father, give me a grateful heart so that I can praise you and be thankful in any circumstance. Thank you, Lord. In Jesus name, I pray, Amen.

*   *   *   *   *

Read Romans 2.

Father God, forgive me for judging others. Thank you for your mercy and grace that allow me to repent and give my life over to you.

Holy Spirit lead me and show me where in my life I need to change.

Heavenly Father, lead me and show me how to deal with any sins in my life. I turn it over to you and ask for forgiveness.

Father, I thank you for eternal life, and I pray that you lead me to obey your will. Father, I thank you that you commanded us to love the Lord thy God with all thy heart, soul, mind, and strength and to love thy neighbor as thyself.

Remind me, O God, that I cannot please you unless I have a proper relationship with you.

Holy Spirit, lead me to look at myself and see if sins of any form exist within me, and turn it over to you, Father, and pray for forgiveness.

I pray that my life will reflect God's love for others. I pray that you will be pleased with how I represent you.

I thank you for circumcising my heart and bringing me into the family of God.

Father God, I pray for stillness so that I can focus on you and your Word. I pray that I will rest in your presence. Change my thoughts and help me view things more biblically.

Thank you that your Word is a lamp to my feet and a light to my path. Thank you, Father God, that I belong to you. You are a good father, in Jesus name, Amen.

* * * * *

My sheep hear my voice, and I know
them, and they follow me. (John 10:27)

Eternal Father, I thank you that I was created to hear you.

As I enter into your rest, Lord, I pray the Holy Spirit leads me to give my body, soul, and mind to Jesus Christ. Holy Spirit, lead me to see the cross each day with a sense of gratitude.

Loving Father, thank you for your son and what he has done for me on the cross. May my life be a living testimony to honoring you and giving you glory.

Holy Spirit, lead me to live each day in faith and obedience to my Lord and Savior, Jesus Christ.

Thank you, Lord, in Jesus name, Amen.

* * * * *

Holy Spirit, help me that my thoughts will be pure, loving, and good. Holy Father, change me from the inside out. May I grow in knowledge of the scriptures. May I be strong spiritually as my relationship with you strengthens.

Help me, Lord Jesus, to set my mind on things above.

Thank you, Father, that the angels of God surround me and protect me and my family.

I declare victory over my life in Jesus name, in the mighty name of Jesus, our Lord and Savior, Amen.

* * * * *

Read Ephesians 4.

Father God, I thank you for choosing me to represent your son, Jesus Christ, on earth.

I pray in the name of Jesus to walk in the fruit of the Spirit so that others will see Christ in me. Holy Spirit, lead me to keep the unity of the Spirit in the bond of peace.

I thank you, Lord, that you are all in all; there is no one else like you. Thank you, God, for sending your son to redeem us from all sins. Thank you, Lord, that you are over the universe, past, present, and future. Nothing is hidden from you because of the spiritual gift you have given me. Lead me to use my gift to glorify and honor you.

Holy Spirit, lead me to speak truth in love. Holy Spirit, lead me to use the new way of thinking that the Heavenly Father has given me. Holy Spirit, lead me to abandon the old ways of life. Lead me to put on the new nature and dress in holiness and righteousness.

Holy Spirit, thank you for renewing the spirit of my mind day by day. I thank you that whatever comes out of my mouth is with grace and seasoned with salt.

Holy Spirit, lead me to be kind to one another, tender-hearted, and forgiving to one another, even as God in Christ Jesus forgave me.

Thank you, Lord, in Jesus name, Amen.

* * * * *

Read Ezekiel 1–3.

Father God, I thank you that your sovereign strength always prevails, and you will judge the enemies and restore your people.

Thank you, Lord, that your presence is everywhere and that you see everything. Thank you that your activities in heaven are shaping events on earth. Thank you, Lord, that you controlled the future.

Holy Father, as you show Ezekiel, Moses, and other prophets your glory, I pray that you will show me your glory.

Ezekiel fell face down, overwhelmed by the contrast between your holiness and his sinfulness. I pray, O Lord, that I will fall on my face before you in reverence and awe of your mercy and grace toward us. Holy Father, as Ezekiel sees the rainbow, it reminds us of your never-ending faithfulness toward us.

Thank you for saving us and choosing to put your breath within us.

The Spirit of the Living God shows us each day that we were made to serve you and give you glory. Holy Spirit, lead me to serve you with all my heart, soul, mind, and strength.

Heavenly Father, as you filled Ezekiel with your Spirit and gave him the power to do the job you sent him to do, I pray that you will empower me to do your will.

Holy Spirit, lead me to be willing and obedient. Holy Spirit, lead me to confess all my sins each day and live to please God in obedience.

Father God, thank you for reminding me not to be afraid or discouraged. Thank you, Lord, for your Spirit, which keeps me so I can lay aside fear, rejection, or ridicule.

Thank you for your powerful strength, which helps me live for you in every situation.

Holy Father, I thank you for your living Word. Lead me to eat your Word so that I can be spiritually fed. Thank you for your words that are sweet like honey. Holy Spirit, lead me to digest God's Word, which will make me strong in my faith. Holy Father, let your Word permeate me.

Thank you, Lord, that I have nothing to fear because your hold on me is strong. Holy Father, I recognized my helplessness before you. I come face down in your presence, Holy Father.

Lord, I need you to help me, lead me, guide me, and strengthen me.

Thank you, Father. I rejoice in you. I pray in Jesus name, Amen.

* * * * *

Read Exodus 33.

Father God, you talk to Moses face-to-face as a friend. Father God, Moses relied wholeheartedly on you for wisdom and direction. Friendship with you, Lord, is a privilege for Moses and also a privilege for me. Thank you, Lord Jesus.

In John 15:15, you call me a friend. I accept the invitation from Father God to openly communicate with you. Thank you, Lord, for your desire to have a relationship with me.

O Heavenly Father, my desire, my hunger, and my thirst are to have an intimate relationship with you.

Heavenly Father, as Moses asked to see your glory, Father God, show me your glory. Holy Spirit, lead me to stay in the presence of God.

Thank you that I see your glory every day through Jesus Christ. Amen.

* * * * *

Heavenly Father, I thank you for having good, pleasing, and perfect plans for your children. I come to you through the mercies of God and present my body as a living sacrifice. I lay aside my own desires and trust in you, Lord, in obedience.

Thank you, Lord, for transforming me with a new mind. Lead me, O Lord, to honor and to obey and to serve you. Thank you for giving us your son to make our new life possible.

I joyfully give my life to you, Lord, and surrender all to you.

Holy Father, transform me into a new person. Change the way I think and let my thoughts be your thoughts. Thank you for giving me the mind of Jesus Christ.

Holy Spirit redirect my mind to the way God created me to be.

Father God, you make it clear in your Word that obedience from the heart is better than sacrifice. Holy Father, circumcise my heart to be obedient to you.

Father God, I pray for humility to lead me to be humble and not to think of myself as better than others.

Thank you, Lord, for the measure of faith that you have given to us. Holy Spirit, lead me to cling to what is good and be kind and affectionate to one another.

I pray that I will be fervent in the spirit, serving the Lord.

Spirit of God, lead me to always rejoice, pray, and worship you.

Holy Spirit, keep my mouth from speaking evil and lead me to live peacefully with everyone.

Father, in the name of Jesus, I turn everything over to you for in your Word it is written that vengeance is yours. "You will repay," says the Lord. Holy Spirit, lead me to do good to others.

Father, I thank you that nothing is impossible for you. I thank you that I can do all things through Christ, who strengthens me.

Thank you, Father God. You are a good father, in Jesus name, Amen.

* * * * *

Father God, as David cried out to you, David longed for a friend. We can trust a father who cares. As a daughter of the Most High God, I cry out to you, "O God. You are my God. Early will I seek you? My soul thirsts for you. My flesh longs for you. In a dry and thirsty land where there is no water. So I have looked for you in the sanctuary to see your power and your glory. Because your love is better than life, my lips shall praise you. O Lord, I will bless you while I live. I will lift up my hands in your name. My soul shall be satisfied, and my mouth shall praise you with joyful lips. When I remember you on my bed, I meditate on you in the night. Because you have been my help, therefore, in the shadow of your wings, I will rejoice. My soul follows close behind you. Your right hand upholds me. Thank you, Lord, that those who seek my life will be destroyed. I rejoice in you, Lord" (Psalm 63:1–11).

I praise you. I worship you. I glorify you. I love you, Lord. In Jesus name, I pray, Amen.

* * * * *

Heavenly Father, I thank you and praise you for calling me out of darkness and into your marvelous light and into your royal family. Thank you for clothing me with your personal robe of righteousness and making me fit for your kingdom.

Father God, thank you that I am one of your own special people. Thank you that I belong to you and that you delight in me.

Holy Spirit, lead me to stay close to my Lord and Savior in everything and consciously rely on you for help.

Lord, lead me to sing praises to you every day in every situation so I can experience your holy power and blessing.

Holy Spirit, lead me to have a heart of gratitude. Holy Father, help me to sing with all my heart so I can feel your presence.

> Let my mouth be filled with your
> praise and with your glory all day. (Psalm
> 71:8)

In Jesus name, I pray, Amen.

*   *   *   *   *

1 Thessalonians 4:9–12

Dear Heavenly Father, I am often tempted to interfere in other people's business and criticize how they are doing things. I pray that my primary focus is to live a life that is faithful to you and that your light will shine to the world around us so that you may be seen and celebrated by all.

Holy Father, when I make mistakes, please allow me to experience godly sorrow, the kind that leads me away from bad decisions and back to you. Give me the courage to repent when I mess up and to choose an abundant life.

Father God, I pray that you will remove the scale from my eyes so that I can see you clearly and be reminded of Jesus Word.

When he says anyone who sees him has seen the father. Holy Spirit, remind me of the comforting Word of Jesus on that day, you will know that I am with my father and you are with me and I am with you.

Glory be to God. Thank you, Lord. Keep my eyes on you, Lord. In Jesus name, I pray, Amen.

*   *   *   *   *

> When Abram was ninety-nine years
> old, the Lord appeared to him and spoke
> to him, "I am almighty God; walk before
> me and be blameless." (Genesis 17:1)

Father God, I thank you that you are El-Shaddai (Almighty God). Father God, I thank you that the same message you had for Abram is the same message you have for us today.

Holy Father, lead me to walk in obedience in every aspect because you are God. You are the only one with the power and ability to change things and meet our every need.

Heavenly Father, lead me to fall on my face before you, be still, and listen to you as you talk to me. Heavenly Father, I thank you that you sanctified me, you redeemed me, and I belong to you.

I pray in the name of Jesus that you will circumcise my heart in obedience to you in everything and every way.

Lord, cut away the old life of sin and purify my heart as I dedicate myself to you.

Holy Spirit, lead me to focus on God's promises for me, follow through, and complete the task that you have given me to do.

Thank you, Lord. I love you, Lord, in Jesus name, Amen.

* * * * *

> There is no fear in love, but perfect
> love casts out fear because fear involves
> torment.
> But he who fears has not been made
> perfect in love. (1 John 4:18)

Merciful God, thank you for loving me. Please fill me with your presence, casting out every fear and transforming me. Hold me in your loving arms, and never let me go. In Jesus sweet name, I pray, Amen.

* * * * *

> Why are you cast down, O my soul,
> and why are you disquited within me?
> Hope in God; for I shall yet praise
> him the help of my countenance and my
> God. (Psalm 43:5)

Dear God, thank you for believing I am worth loving. Keep me from despair. Help me put my whole trust in you. My life is in your hands.

Thank you, my savior, my helper, my God, my redeemer, my provider, and my everything. Thank you, Lord, in Jesus name, Amen.

* * * * *

> Casting all your care upon him
> because he cares for you. (1 Peter 5:7)

Lord Jesus, I pray that you will show me when I am carrying too much. Help me, Lord, to cast all my burdens over to you. Help me to find rest for my weary soul.

Lord, help me not to be anxious. Lord, lead me to stay on the course that you have set for me. Thank you, Lord, that your timing is perfect.

Lord, lead me to surrender to the warmth of your welcoming arms and the wisdom of your ways.

The Spirit of God dwells in me. Lead me to soak in your presence. Here I am, Lord, and you can have it all. Everything is yours, Lord Jesus. In Jesus name, I pray, Amen.

* * * * *

Thank you for welcoming me with open arms because I am a child of God through our union with our Lord and Savior, Jesus Christ.

Father God, I thank you that I can talk to you about everything. Thank you for listening to me. Thank you, Lord, that you give me your love and power. Thank you for being my father and the rightful owner of everything.

Help me, Lord, to stay in contact with other believers in the body of Christ.

Thank you, Lord, that your love is wide and reaches out to the whole world. God's love is long. It extends throughout our lives and into eternity. God's love is high. It rises to the heights. God's love is deep. It reaches to the depths of discouragement. I thank you, Lord, that I am complete in you. In you, Lord, I lack nothing, nothing is lost, and nothing to fear.

I have all the fullness of God available to me. Holy Spirit, lead me to claim the fullness of God through faith and prayer each day. Holy Spirit, fill every aspect of my life to the fullest, in Jesus name, Amen.

* * * * *

> For the word of God is living, powerful, and sharper than any two-edged sword, piercing even to the division of soul and spirit and of joints and marrow, and is a discerner of the thoughts and intents of the heart. (Hebrews 4:12)

Lord, I believe without a doubt that you are a good father. Yet sometimes I still feel afraid. In those times, I remember that I am not approaching the throne of God alone.

The King of kings and the Lord of lords take my hand and lead me forward. What a relief to know that Jesus intercedes and claims me as his own.

When my voice cracks and I stumble over words, Jesus speaks with authority and conviction. When I pour out my failure, Jesus announces forgiveness.

Lord, as I come to you with my petition, I know that there is no better advocate willing to fight for me than Jesus.

Lord, as I come boldly to the throne of grace, I thank you for your grace and mercy in my time of need. I love you, Lord. In Jesus's name, I pray, amen.

* * * * *

Father, thank you that you called me into this intimate relationship with Jesus.

Help me to put my roots down deep and to keep my eyes fixed on you. Help me to guard this relationship and never allow other things, even good things, to crowd in and change my life.

Holy Spirit, lead me into a stillness in the presence of God. In Jesus name, I pray, Amen.

* * * * *

Read Jude 1.

Lord, I give you thanks. I glorify and honor you. Holy Spirit, lead me to be more like Jesus every day.

I thank you that I've been called by God the Father, who loves me and keeps me safe in the care of Jesus Christ. Lord, I thank you for the mercy, peace, and love that you store in me. Lord, I thank you for your love letter that showed me how to live a godly life.

Holy Spirit, lead me to walk in faith. Lead me to be bold and defend my faith that God has entrusted to me, his daughter. Holy Spirit, lead me to stay away from earthly desires and stay in the will of God. Holy Spirit, lead me to have a heart of gratitude and live only to please God.

I pray that we will build each other up in the most holy faith. Lord, I pray that you lead me to pray in the power of the Holy Spirit and await the mercy of our Lord Jesus Christ, who will bring us eternal life. In this way, we will keep ourselves safe in God's love.

Lord, lead me to show mercy to those whose faith is wavering.

Holy Spirit, lead me to hate sin.

All glory to God, who is able to keep me from falling and bring me great joy in his glorious presence. All glory to him who alone is God our savior through Jesus Christ our Lord. All glory, majesty, power, and authority are his before all time, in the present, and beyond all time, in Jesus name, Amen.

* * * *

Read Psalm 66.

Lord, I sing joyful praise to you, my God. Lord, I sing about the glory of your name. Lord, lead me to tell the world how glorious you are.

How awesome are your deeds? Everyone bows down before your mighty power, and everything on earth will worship you. They will sing your praise and shout your name in glorious song.

Lord, I praise you for your awesome miracles. You have performed for your people. You made a dry path through the Red Sea, and your people went across on foot. Lord, we rejoice in you, O God, and loudly sing your praise. My life is in your hands.

Lord, I thank you for keeping my feet from stumbling. Lord, thank you for purifying us as silver and bringing us to a place of great abundance. Lord, I come to you as a living sacrifice.

I pray that you will lead me, Holy Spirit, to fear the Lord and to listen as you speak.

Lord, I thank you that I can cry out for help and that you hear from me.

Holy Father, I praise you. Lord, I confessed all my sins. Thank you for listening and paying attention to my prayer. Lord, I praise and worship you for hearing my prayer. Thank you for your unfailing love. In Jesus name, I pray, Amen.

*   *   *   *   *

Dear God, thank you for the cross of Jesus. Holy Spirit, lead me to put my past behind me and know that I have victory because of the finished work on the cross.

Holy Father, if I am harboring bitterness or wrong feelings toward someone today, Lord, I pray that you help me to take the step to make things right with them.

Father God, please give me the courage to embrace them and show them grace, mercy, and forgiveness.

Lord, make me a healer and reconciler. Just as you are the great healer and reconciler, Lord, lead me to dedicate my life to you every day. Thank you, Lord, for calling me your daughter. Thank you for the fact that I belong to you.

Help me, Lord, to always place my trust in you. In Jesus name, I pray, Amen.

*   *   *   *   *

Lord, I submit myself to you. Quicken my conscience with your holiness. Nourish my mind with your truth. Purify my imagination with your beauty. Open my heart to your love. I surrender my all to your purpose. I worship and adore you, in Jesus's name, amen.

* * * * *

But you shall receive power when
the Holy Spirit has come upon you, and
you shall be witnesses to me in Jerusalem,
in all Judea and Samaria, and to the end
of the earth. (Acts 1:8)

Holy God in heaven, please give me the courage to share the message of the Gospel with the people I meet: strangers, family, and friends. Fill me with the power of the Holy Spirit and help me to be a faithful witness for you. In the name of Jesus, I pray, amen.

* * * * *

Now hope does not disappoint
because the love of God has been poured
out in our hearts by the Holy Spirit, who
was given to us. (Romans 5:5)

Lord, I thank you for giving me the Holy Spirit to live in me and to be with me forever. Thank you for giving me your peace, and you promise to answer my prayers. Help me to follow the obedience and humility of Jesus.

May the spirit of the truth lead and guide me and give me your peace.

Lord, help me to follow Jesus's examples, not just in words but also in actions.

Thank you for giving us so much to celebrate. Lord, I thank you for all the great things you have done for me.

Lord, please give me a heart like yours, a heart of love. Help me to trust in your unfailing love.

Thank you that your love is poured into my heart by the Holy Spirit, who has been given to me. Lord, please pour your love into my heart today, in Jesus's name, amen.

* * * * *

Peace, I leave with you; my peace I
give to you, not as the world gives, but as
I give to you.
Let not your heart be troubled, nor
let it be afraid. (John 14:27)

Lord, help me to be a person who promotes peace and who speaks words of healing, truth, and kindness.

Lord, I thank you that I can live in peace, knowing that in everything you work for the good of those who love you.

Lord, I commit myself to you again to serve you only.

Forgive my sins and the sins of the world. I cry out for your deliverance and peace.

May we see many people in this land putting their faith in Jesus and finding peace in every situation. I pray in the name of Jesus, Amen.

* * * * *

Lord, I thank you that I can come to you and pour out my heart to you, knowing that you are listening.

I thank you for being in control of every situation. I will rejoice in the Lord. I will be joyful in God, my savior. Lord, I thank you that I can find hope and help in your presence.

Thank you, Lord, for being my strength. You are the only one who can satisfy my soul. I rejoice in you, Lord. In Jesus name, I pray, Amen.

* * * * *

> But the fruit of the spirit is love, joy, peace, longsuffering, kindness, goodness, faithfulness, gentleness, and self-control Against such, there is no law
>
> And those who are Christ have crucified the flesh with it passions and desires.
>
> If we live in the spirit, let us also walk in the spirit. (Galatians 5:22–25)

Lord, I commit my life to you and surrender to your will. Lord, I thank you that there is power in the name of Jesus. Lord, sometimes I am not living according to the fruit of the Spirit. I pray that you will forgive me, Lord. I pray for an opportunity today to show the fruit of the Spirit to everyone.

Lord Jesus, I pray that you will open the eyes of my heart to better see the glory of God's grace. Lord, fill me with streams of living water. Lord, I pray that you will satisfy my thirst, break every bondage, and help me be like Jesus, to demonstrate not only the power of the Spirit but also the fruit of the wonderful Holy Spirit in my daily life. In Jesus name, I pray, Amen.

* * * * *

> And they were all filled with the
> Holy Spirit and began to speak in other
> tongues as the Spirit gave them utter-
> ance. (Act 2:4)

Lord, I thank you for who you are, my Savior and King. Lord, whatever my circumstances are, help me to praise your name in song and glorify you with thanksgiving. Lord, I pray for a fresh outpouring of the Holy Spirit.

May the fire of God descend upon me, the church, and my family again with power, passion, and purity. Lord, may the churches again be filled with the sound of worship and celebration. May every day be filled with the sound of the Pentecostal outpouring of the Holy Spirit to the glory of your name. Thank you, Father God. In Jesus name, Amen.

* * * * *

> The steadfast love of the Lord never
> ceases; these mercies never come to an
> end; they are new every morning.
> Great is your faithfulness; the Lord
> is my portion, says my soul; therefore,
> I will have faith in him. (Lamentations
> 3:22–24)

Lord, I thank you for that outpouring of grace that greeted me every day. Lord, I thank you for your promises that when I repent of my sins, you will forgive me. Lord, I repent all the sins I ever committed. I pray for your forgive-ness in Jesus name.

Father God, I pray that in moments of conflict, I will call upon you for help to slowly speak, slow to get angry, and quick to listen.

Lord, lead me to love those who frustrate me. Lord, sometimes my emotions get in the way. Lord, I pray that you will help me to always be wise with my words so that I can be a good representation of our Lord and Savior, Jesus Christ. In Jesus name, I pray, Amen.

* * * * *

But you have an anointing from
the Holy One, and you know all things.
(1 John 2:20)

Lord, help me to follow Jesus, whom God anointed with the Holy Spirit and power. Lord, whatever I face in life, I pray for the power and anointing of the Holy Spirit. Lord, I pray that you will lead me to walk in the will of God. Lord, help me to be strong and to walk faithfully before you with all my heart and soul. Lord, I praise your Holy name. In Jesus name, I pray, Amen.

* * * * *

Father God, I thank you for this new day. Holy Spirit, I pray that you will lead me to put my trust and my life in the Lord Jesus Christ so I can discover his unfailing love shining on me in the midst of every situation I face.

Lord, I trust you will lead me to say it over and over again. Lord, I trust you. Lord, you are the creator and sustainer of the universe. You are my Lord and Savior. You are my friend and king.

Thank you, Lord, that your love never runs out or grows old. Thank you that you are the same yesterday, today, and forever, as is your perfect love for me.

Lord, I lift my soul to you, waiting in your presence with a hungry heart. Lord, I worship you and praise your Holy name. Lord, show me the way to go throughout this day and always. Lord, I trust you wholeheartedly.

Thank you for taking care of me. Thank you for saving me. I rejoice in you, Lord. In Jesus name, I pray, Amen.

* * * * *

> I beseech you therefore, brethren, by the mercies of God, that you present your bodies as a living sacrifice, holy and acceptable to God, which is your reasonable service.
>
> And do not be conformed to this world, but be transformed by the renewing of your mind, that you may prove what is the good, acceptable, and perfect will of God. (Romans 12:1–2)

Lord, I thank you that you have a good, pleasing, and perfect plan for me. Holy Spirit, lead me to lay aside my own desires and follow you. Lord, I trust you to guide me. Thank you for taking away all my sins and setting me free.

Father God, I pray that you will transform me into a new person by changing the way I think. Lord, I need more than anything to please you and do your will. Holy Spirit, I pray for strength and courage to fulfill your calling for my life. Thank you, Lord. In Jesus name, I pray, Amen.

* * * * *

> I will love you, O Lord, my strength.
> The Lord is my rock, my fortress,
> and my stronghold.
> My God, my strength in whom I
> will trust.
> My shield, the horn of my salvation,
> and my stronghold. (Psalm 18:1–2)

Lord, I thank you that you are my strength, my rock, my fortress, and my deliverer. Lord, I pray that you will deliver me from sin and from my own prideful self. Please prepare the way before me and help me follow where you lead.

Holy Father, thank you for trusting me to spread the good news of your great love. Help me to proclaim your good news wherever I am. Thank you, Lord, for loving me. In Jesus name, Amen.

* * * * *

> I am confident in this very thing:
> that he who has begun a good work in
> me will complete it until the day of Jesus
> Christ. (Philippians 1:6)

Father God, I thank you. I worship you and praise your Holy name. Lord, as the beginning of the day started, I turn it over to you. I turn my heart, soul, body, mind, and spirit to you, Lord Jesus.

Lord, for the past few weeks, I have been reflecting on the past hurt and pain. Dear God of heaven, please help me to overcome the things the enemy throws at me. I humbly ask for your guidance and protection.

Lord, I pray that you will show me the pathway you want me to take. Lord, I pray for forgiveness. Lord, I need your help to let go. I repented of all my sins, and I pray that you will change me and lead me to live a life the way you created me to be. In the mighty name of Jesus, I pray, Amen.

* * * * *

I sought the Lord, and he heard
me and delivered me from all my fears.
(Psalm 34:4)

Lord, I cry to you for help. In the morning, my prayer comes before you. O Lord, I spread out my hands to you. I asked you for help. Lord, I cry out to you for your help. Please fill me with your Holy Spirit today. I really need the help of the Holy Spirit to live the kind of life that you call me to live.

Lord, I want not only to know you but also to press on to know you better. I cry to you from my heart for healing, restoration, and revival. Holy Father, I receive your strength. I worship you, O Lord. Thank you, Lord, in the name of Jesus, my Lord and Savior, King of kings, and Lord of lords. In Jesus name, I pray, Amen.

* * * * *

Praise the Lord! For it is good to
sing praises to our God.

For it is pleasant, and praise is beautiful. (Psalm 147:1)

O Lord, my God, may I praise you forever and ever.
You, O Lord, are great in your power, your glory, your victory, and your majesty. Everything in heaven and on earth
belongs to you. I adore you, Lord, as one who is over all
things. Wealth and honor come from you alone for you rule
over everything. Power and might are in your hands.

Lord, I thank you for your strength. Lord, I thank you
and praise your glorious name. Lord, everything we have is
a blessing from you, and we give you what you have first
given us. Lord, I honor your Holy name. Lord, thank you for
examining my heart and rejoice when you find a clean heart.

O Lord, the God of Abram, Isaac, and Jacob, make me
always want to obey you and serve you.

Lord, I pray that you will lead me to always love you
with all my heart, soul, mind, and strength and to love my
neighbors as myself.

Lord, I pray that you give me a wholehearted desire
to always please you. Lord, I give you praise. I worship and
rejoice in you. All these things I pray, in the name of Jesus,
my Lord and Savior. Amen.

* * * * *

Rejoice always.
Pray without ceasing.
In everything, give thanks, for this
is the will of God in Christ Jesus for you.
(1 Thessalonians 5:16–18)

Dear God, I don't want to be so shortsighted that I fail to see all you do for me. Please led me to be aware every day of the gifts you have given me and be thankful.

Lord, lead me to have a grateful heart and reach out to others in love. Lord, please help me to remember that all I have is yours. Help me share it willingly with others without complaining.

Holy Spirit, lead me to have a heart of gratitude. Holy Spirit, I pray that you will lead me to have a praying spirit, seeking the Lord and staying in his presence. Thank you, Lord, and I rejoice in you. In Jesus name, I pray, Amen.

* * * *

Lord, I cry out to you.
Make haste for me.
Give ear to my voice. (Psalm 141:1)

When I cry out to you, Lord, let my prayer be set before you as a living sacrifice and lifting up my hands in worship.

Lord, I pray that you will set a guard over my mouth and keep watch over the door of my lips.

Holy Father, I pray that you will lead my heart, my speech, and my actions back to you the way you created me to be.

Holy Spirit, I pray that you will keep my eyes on you.

Lord, in you I take refuge. You are my strength, O Lord. Thank you, Lord, in Jesus name, Amen.

* * * *

I have come down from heaven.
Not to do my own will but the will
of him who sent me. (John 6:38)

Heavenly Father, you demonstrated your great love to us by giving us your one and only son to save and redeem us.

Lord, thank you that in the ultimate act of service, you took upon yourself the curse that should have fallen on us. Thank you that as a result, I am justified by faith in you. Thank you for setting me free.

Lord Jesus, thank you that you alone fulfilled the prophecy perfectly and that you will not give your glory to another.

Thank you for your model of humility and gentleness. Thank you for calling me to be a servant of the Lord.

Lord, I pray that you will lead me to follow your example and that others will see Christ in me.

Thank you, Lord, in Jesus name, Amen.

* * * * *

Oh, give thanks to the Lord, for he is good.

His mercy endures forever. (Psalm 107:1)

Lord, I thank you for another day. Holy Spirit, I pray that you will help me get through this day praising you and worshipping your Holy name.

Lord, I choose to walk with you along the path of peace. Lord, I lean on you as my refuge and my strength. Lord, I thank you that you transform trials into blessings. Lord, I cry out to you for your help. Lord, as I turn toward you, I pray that the light of your presence shine upon me.

Thank you, Lord, in Jesus name, Amen.

* * * * *

> But seek first the kingdom of God
> and his righteousness, and all these things
> shall be added to you. (Matthew 6:33)

Lord, I pray that you will lead me to seek the kingdom of God above all else and live righteously. Holy Spirit, lead me to put God first in my life and to fill my thoughts with these desires.

Lord, lead me to use your character as a life pattern and keep on implementing your kingdom values on earth.

Holy Spirit, lead me to give God first place in every area of my life. Lead me to maintain a good relationship with God, loving God with all my heart, soul, mind, and strength and loving others as myself.

These things I ask in the mighty name of Jesus, my Lord and King, Amen.

* * * * *

> But the Lord said to Samuel: "Do
> not look at his appearance or his physical
> stature. Because I have refused him. For
> the Lord does not see as man sees. Man
> looks at the outward appearance, but the
> Lord looks at the heart." (1 Samuel 16:7)

Lord, I thank you for seeing beyond the outward appearance. Thank you, Lord, that you see into my heart. Lord, I pray that my face will reflect the love and joy you put into my heart.

Lord, I pray that you will lead me to bring encouragement and confidence to everyone I encounter. Lord, I thank you for the inspiring example of those like Apostle Paul.

Whatever the outward appearance or circumstance, may my heart be full of joy. May I not judge people or situations by how they look from the outside, but like you, Jesus, always to look at the heart.

Lord, my heart is turned toward you, yet you know how often I fail. Please forgive me and have mercy on me.

Thank you, Lord, that you enable me to turn back to you each day. Thank you for filling my heart with joy and helping me to follow you wholeheartedly today and always. Thank you, Lord, that you hear the cry of my heart. Thank you that there is now no condemnation for those who are in Christ Jesus. Thank you, Lord, that all your words must come to pass. Thank you for your living Word, in Jesus name, Amen.

* * * * *

Preserve me, O God, for in you I
put my trust. You are my Lord.
My goodness is nothing apart from
you. (Psalm 16:1–2)

Lord, I thank you that you are my Lord and Master, and you have rightful authority over my life. Lord, I thank you that I was created for your glory.

And I belong to you, and everything I have belongs to you. Thank you, Lord, that you created me out of love so I can put you first in every aspect of my life and give you complete allegiance.

Father God, I come to you seeking your will for my life.

Lord, I pray that you will give me insights that will help me make godly decisions and live according to your will. Lord, I give you total control of my life as I communicate with you and allow you to counsel me and give me wisdom. Lord, I thank you for the resurrection power of Jesus Christ.

I thank you that the same power is in me. Glory be to God! I thank you because I will not be shaken. I thank you that you are at the right hand of the Father, and I will not be moved from your chosen path.

Lord, I thank you that my heart is glad and that my spirit rejoices in you. My flesh will also rest in hope. Lord, I thank you that the secret of joy is in you. Lord, I thank you for your daily presence, where I find joy, love, peace, and contentment. Lord, I thank you for showing me the path of life. In your presence is fullness of joy. At your right hand are pleasures forever more. All glory and honor to you, Lord, in Jesus name, Amen.

* * * * *

Let your speech always be with grace
and salt, so that you may know how you
ought to answer each one. (Colossians 4:6)

Lord, I pray for a new refreshing of the Holy Spirit this day and always. I pray that you will help me to let my speech always be with grace and salt so that I may know how to answer each one, in Jesus name, Amen.

* * * * *

If you keep my commandments,
you will abide in my love.
Just as I have kept my Father's commandments and abided in his love

> These things I have spoken to you
> so that my joy may remain in you and
> that your joy be full. (John 15:10–11)

Lord, I thank you, I praise you, and I glorify your Holy name. Lord, I pray that you will lead me to keep your commandments and abide in your love. Lord, I thank you that the joy of living with Jesus Christ daily will keep me level-headed in every circumstance. Lord, I pray that you will give me the desire and the ability to do what you call me to do. Lord, I surrender all to you.

I thank you for saving me, for fixing me, for changing me, for healing me, for helping me, and for making me more like Jesus each day.

Dear God, I offer you my heart. Thank you for never leaving me or forsaking me. Help me to live like the treasure that I am to you. In Jesus mighty name, I pray, Amen.

* * * * *

> He will cover you with his feathers.
> And under his wings you shall take
> refuge.
> His truth shall be your shield and
> buckler. (Psalm 91:4)

Lord Jesus, I pray that you will lead me to stay close to you. Thank you for being my protector and for pointing me to where I find my soul nourishment.

Lord, I pray that you will shade me from the excess heat of life and warm me with your closeness. Thank you, Lord, for sheltering me beneath your wings. In Jesus Holy name, I pray, Amen.

* * * * *

Lord, I thank and praise you for broadening the path beneath me so I do not fall. Thank you, Lord, that you know the beginning and the end. Thank you for being a loving father who is involved in my life. Lord, I thank you for the cross. Thank you for setting us free. Thank you for your promise that you will always be with us. All glory and honor to you, Lord Jesus, in Jesus name, Amen.

* * * * *

Lord Jesus, I believe in you, and I believe in the one who sent you. When I see you, I see the Father who sent you. Thank you for coming into this world to save us so that we can see the Father more clearly. Thank you, Jesus, that you and the Father are one.

Lord, I pray that I will set my eyes on you. Thank you that the Father, Son, and Holy Spirit are gifts to me. Thank you, Lord, that we can pray to the Father in the name of Jesus. Thank you, Jesus. Thank you, Holy Spirit, in Jesus name, Amen.

* * * * *

Lord, I thank you for the cross. Thank you for giving us yourself. Thank you, Lord, that all the treasures of wisdom and knowledge are hidden in you.

Lord, open wide my heart, mind, and spirit to receive you in full measure. Lord, thank you that the light of your presence shines upon me. I look to you, Lord, with a trusting heart.

Holy Spirit, lead me to seek you and thank you for the joy of your light that breaks through the dark.

Lord, I pray that your heavenly light will soak into me and fill me. In the name of Jesus, I pray, Amen.

* * * * *

Lord, I thank you for blessing me with your grace and peace. Lord, I open my heart and mind to receive all that you have for me.

Lord, I thank you that you know me and that you can see straight through me into the depths of my being. Lord, as I come to you, I pray that you will transform my weaknesses into strengths. Lord, I thank you that my relationship with you is saturated in grace. Lord, I thank you that nothing can separate me from your love. Thank you, Lord, for your presence, in Jesus name, Amen.

* * * * *

Cause me to hear your loving kindness in the morning.
For in you do I trust, causing me to
know the way in which I should walk.
I lift up my soul to you. (Psalm
143:8)

Lord, I thank you for shining your face upon me. Thank you for your peace, which transcends all understanding. Lord, I pray that you will lead me to focus on you. Where I can find peace and safety in your presence?

Lord, I thank you that in every circumstance, I can call upon you. Help me, Jesus, and you will lift me up with your hand of righteousness. Lord, lead me to fix my eyes upon you, the one who never changes. Thank you, Lord, in Jesus name, Amen.

* * * * *

Lord, I thank you that you are the living one who sees me always. You see in the depths of my being. You know my thoughts. Lord, I thank you that I am never alone. You are always with me.

Lord, I pray that you will cleanse my heart from any sinful tendencies. Lord, I pray for a repenting heart. Forgive me for all my sins. Lord, thank you for clothing me in your robe of righteousness. Lord, I pray that you will lead me to keep my eyes on you, in Jesus name, Amen.

* * * * *

Lord, I thank you and praise you for you are always with me. Lord, I thank you that before you ascend into heaven, you told us you would be with us always even to the end of the age, and I believe and trust you that you will never leave me or forsake me.

Lord, I pray that my daily life will reflect the life that you call me to live. Thank you, Lord, that you see my heart. Thank you, Lord, that because you are with me, every moment of my life is more meaningful. Lord, I rejoice in you, in Jesus name, Amen.

* * * * *

Heavenly Father, I pray that you will help me keep my focus on you. Thank you for the amazing freedom that you have given me. Lord, I choose your mind. I choose to think the way you think.

Lord, I thank you that I was made in your image to think and do everything according to your glory. Lord, I bring every thought captive to you in Jesus name. Guard me and keep me in constant peace as I focus my mind on you. Lord, be glorified in Jesus name, Amen.

* * * * *

Lord, I thank you and praise you that your compassion never fails; it is new every morning. Great is your faithfulness.

Thank you, Lord, that your reservoir of blessings is full to the brim. In every circumstance, Lord, I wait for you. Lord, as I wait, I drink from your fountain that will never dry up. Thank you, Lord, for the peace that passes all understanding. In Jesus name, I pray, Amen.

* * * * *

Lord, I thank you that you are my rock and my Savior God. Lord, I pray that I will spend time pondering your greatness and your mercy toward me. Lord, I thank you for being my forever friend and the lover of my soul. Thank you, Lord, for your death on the cross. Thank you for saving us, Lord.

Lord, I thank you for your love and your righteousness, which keep us secure in your love. Thank you for your loving words. Thank you that someday we will live with you in paradise. Thank you, Lord, in Jesus name, Amen.

* * * * *

Lord, I thank you that when I wait in your presence, there is peace. Lord, I pray that I will rest in your presence. I pray that you will refresh my soul and give me strength to walk into your will.

Holy Father, lead me to have good courage. Holy Spirit, thank you for leading me to be strong and courageous. Holy Spirit, lead me to discipline myself to fix my eyes and thoughts on the Lord Jesus Christ. Thank you, Father God. In Jesus name, I pray, Amen.

* * * * *

Lord, I thank you for creating me with the ability to communicate with the immortal, invisible King of the universe.

Lord, I thank you for this privilege and this opportunity. Lord Jesus, as you depend on the Father and pray to the Father, I pray that I will depend on the Holy Spirit to lead me in everything I do and say.

Holy Spirit, I pray that you will help me to pray effectively and pray the will of God. Thank you, Lord. In Jesus name, I pray, Amen.

* * * * *

Lord, I look to you and your strength. Lead me to seek your face always.

Lord, I pray for a rejoicing heart as I seek you. Thank you, Lord, for being the lover of my soul.

Lord, I glorify you. You are a holy God. Thank you, Lord Jesus, that I can use your name to worship you and commune with you.

Lord, I thank you as I worship, you delight in me and it brings me joy in my heart. Thank you, Lord, in Jesus's name, Amen.

* * * * *

Lord, I thank you that there is power in your name. Lord Jesus, as I call upon your name, I pray that the light of Jesus will shine on me.

Thank you, Lord, for watching over me and loving me eternally. Lord, I pray that you lead me to return my focus to you. Holy Spirit, saturate my mind and heart with the Word of God. Lead me to read, study, and meditate on the Word of God.

Thank you, Lord, that your Word is a lamp to my feet and a light for my path. Lord, I delight in the joy of your presence, in Jesus name, Amen.

* * * * *

Lord, I thank you for keeping my lamp burning. Thank you for turning my darkness into light. Thank you, Lord, that I can call upon you in every situation. Lord, I thank you for fueling my lamp. You are my strength; you are my light.

Lord, I pray that you will lead me to let the glory of your presence soak into me. Holy Spirit, please lead me to trust the Lord wholeheartedly. Lord, I thank you for transforming me into your will. In Jesus name, I pray, Amen.

* * * * *

Lord Jesus, I pray that I will see myself in your eyes and become more and more like you every day.

Holy Spirit, I pray that you will control my thoughts and behavior to make me more like Jesus. Holy Spirit, lead me to break free from entanglement as I affirm my trust in you.

Lord, lead me to spend time in your presence and enjoy your presence. Lord, lead me to forget about myself and focus on you, my Lord and Savior, as I grow increasingly free. I love you, Lord. In Jesus name, I pray, Amen.

* * * * *

Lord, I thank you for calling me to rest in your presence, where you placed me to be and where I am beloved. Lord, I pray that I will be still in your presence and fix my eyes on you. Holy Spirit, lead me to relax and enjoy the nearness of the Lord. Thank you, Lord, for always being with me.

Lord, as I meditate on you and your Word, I pray that your grace and truth will soak into the depths of my soul and draw me closer to you. Lord, I whisper your name. Jesus, in your sweet remembrance of your nearness, Lord, lead me to put you first in everything I do or say. In Jesus name, I pray, Amen.

* * * * *

Lord, I thank you that I am handpicked for your blessing and growth. Thank you for bringing me into a deep, intimate relationship with you. Lord, lead me to embrace everything that you allow in my life. I trust you to bring good out of them as I rely more fully on you.

Holy Spirit, lead me in a spirit of worshipping and praising, when I am feeling stressed. Let those feelings alert my need for you.

Let my need for you Lord become a doorway to deep dependence on you and increasing intimacy, in Jesus name, Amen.

* * * * *

Taste and see that the Lord is good. Thank you, Lord, for you are a good Father. Thank you for your peace.

Lord, when you appear to the disciples after the resurrection, it was peace that you communicated first of all. Thank you, Lord, that you know me and give me your peace. Your peace calms every fear and clears my mind.

Holy Spirit, I pray that you will lead me to listen to the voice of the Lord and tune out all other voices.

Lord, I thank you that you designed me to dwell in your peace every day and always. Lord, lead me to draw near to you and receive your peace.

In Jesus name, Amen

* * * * *

Lord, as I wait on you, I pray that you will direct my attention to you and lead me to trust you with every fiber of my being.

I thank you, Lord, for creating me to glorify you and stay conscious of you as I go about my daily duties. Lord, I thank you for enabling me to glorify you by living in deep dependence on you, ready to do your will.

Lord, lead me to enjoy your presence in fullness of joy, worshipping and glorifying you. In Jesus name, I pray, Amen.

* * * * *

Lord, I thank you that I was created for your glory. Lord, I pray for a thankful heart and a thankful mindset that keeps me connected to you.

Lord, I pray for a heart of gratitude and that you will lead me to cultivate a thankful heart that glorifies you and fills me with joy and peace.

> Enter his gates with thanksgiving
> and his courts with praise.
> Give thanks to him and praise his
> name. (Psalm 100:4)

In Jesus name, Amen.

* * * * *

Lord, I thank you for speaking to me from the depths of my being and saying smooth words of peace and love to me. Lord, I thank you for the Holy Spirit that takes charge of my mind and transforms me through your truth. Lord, I pray for the light of your presence as it shines upon me always. Lord, I thank you that I am fully equipped to be holy because you dwell in me.

Thank you, Lord, that you have clothed me with the garments of salvation and covered me with the robe of righteousness, in Jesus name, Amen.

* * * * *

Lord, I come to you for wisdom, knowledge, understanding, discernment, and revelation. Lord, I thank you that you know me better than I know myself and that no detail of my life is hidden from you.

Thank you, Lord, that you view me through the eyes of grace. Lord, I thank you for your intimate awareness. Lord, I thank you for the light of your healing presence that shines into the deepest recesses of my being.

Lord, I thank you for your Holy Spirit, who comforts me. Thank you, Lord, for cleansing, healing, refreshing, and renewing me. Thank you, Lord, for forgiving me of all my sins, in Jesus name, Amen.

* * * * *

Holy Father, as I come to you, I pray that you will lead me to rest in your radiant presence, where there is a cushion of calmness.

Holy Spirit, I pray that you will lead me into the smoothing center, where I will be energized and filled with love, joy, and peace.

Lord, I pray that you will lead me to depend on you alone. Lord, saturate me with your power so that I can be what you created me to be. Lord, lead me in the light of your presence that others will see Jesus in me, in Jesus name, Amen.

* * * * *

Lord, I thank you and praise your Holy name. I thank you that you reside in the deepest depths of my being in eternal union with your Holy Spirit. Lord, I thank you that your peace reigns continually in me and has an eternal grip on me. Thank you, Lord, that you are Christ in me, the hope of glory.

> Nor height, nor depth, nor any other created thing shall be able to separate us from the love of God, which is in Christ Jesus our Lord. (Romans 8:39)

Thank you, Lord. I love you, Lord, in Jesus name, Amen.

* * * * *

Father God, I thank you for the risen savior who shines upon me always. Lord, I pray that you will invade every part of my life. Thank you for making me into a new creation with old things passing away and new things continuing every day. Lord, I embrace all that you are doing in my life.

Holy Spirit, I pray that you will open my eyes to see all that you want me to see. Lord, I am all yours, in Jesus name, Amen.

* * * * *

Lord, I thank you for the conditions that are requiring me to be still. Help me not to spoil these quiet moments by wishing them away.

Lord, lead me to search for your ways in the midst of every circumstance. Lord, I pray that you will lead me to quietness and trust that will enhance my awareness of your presence, strength, and power most effective in my weakness. Thank you, Lord, for your strength and power, in Jesus name, Amen.

Lord, I thank you and worship your Holy name. Lord, I come to you with all my weaknesses: physical, emotional, and spiritual.

Lord, I rest in the comfort of your presence, remembering that nothing is impossible with you. Thank you, Lord, that you are my shepherd.

Lord, I thank you that the safest place to be is in your will. Holy Spirit, I pray that you will lead me into the will of our Lord and Savior, Jesus Christ. Thank you, Lord, in Jesus name, Amen.

* * * * *

Lord, I thank you that I can be confident knowing that your presence is with me all the days of my life. Lord, as I fix my eyes on you, the author and perfector of my faith, I thank you for clearing the way before me.

Thank you, Lord, for holding me with your righteous right hand. Thank you, Lord, that your Word enlightens my mind and heart, empowering me to stay on the right path. Holy Spirit, lead me to stay in the scriptures, which are the words of life. Thank you, Lord, in Jesus name, Amen.

* * * * *

Lord, I thank you for the resurrection power that is in me. Thank you for the peace that is within me. I pray it will settle over me and enfold me in your loving presence.

Lord, I pray that we will wear your peace with dignity and that our hearts and minds will keep close to you.

> You will keep him in perfect peace,
> whose mind stayed on you because he
> trusted in you. (Isaiah 26:3)

Thank you, Lord, in Jesus name, Amen.

* * * * *

Lord, I thank you for always being with me and hovering over me. Lord, you know all my ways and thoughts. I thank you for the Holy Spirit that lives within me and leads me each day to have godly thoughts.

Lord, I pray that I will keep my eyes on you as you lead me into your presence, where I find joy and peace. Lord, I thank you that when you created me, you put a desire in my soul that only you can satisfy. Lord, I delight in you because you are the desire of my heart. Thank you, Lord, in Jesus name, Amen.

* * * * *

Lord, I pray that I will seek your face more and more as you lead me into a deep, intimate relationship with you. Lord, I trust you, and I will not be afraid since you are my strength and song.

> These things I have spoken to you,
> that in me you may have peace. In the
> world, you will have tribulation, but

be of good cheer; I have overcome the
world. (John 16:33)

Thank you, Lord, in Jesus name, Amen.

* * * * *

Lord, I thank you that when I stay in your presence,
I will rise above all circumstances and rest in your heavenly
realms. Thank you, Lord, that the way of peace is living in
the light of your presence.

Lord, as I cry out, help me. I feel your righteous hand
holding me. I pray that your face will shine upon me, blessing me with your peace. In Jesus name, I pray, Amen.

* * * * *

Your ears shall hear a word behind
you, saying, This is the way; walk in it.
Whenever you turn to the right or whenever you turn to the left. (Isaiah 30:21)

Lord, I thank you that the power of Jesus lives in me. I
thank you that I have the ability to live in righteousness and
holiness. I thank you that I have the nature of Jesus Christ
through the power of the Holy Spirit. I thank you that I have
the desire of Jesus in me. Lord Jesus, I want to be more like
you today and always.

Holy Spirit, help me to make every effort to please you
today and to be fruitful, in Jesus name, Amen.

Iverine James is a Christian author who centers her journey of faith, self-discovery, and spiritual growth through the words written in this book. As she navigates through this transformative journey, she examines her values and seeks to reconcile her personal experiences with her religious convictions. Her triumphs in her spiritual exploration ultimately led her to a renewed sense of purpose, connection, and enlightenment. And her experiences serve as an inspiration for readers, inviting them to reflect on their own spiritual paths and seek a more profound connection with Jesus Christ.